START WHERE YOU ARE

START WHERE YOU ARE

My Journey from Childhood Poverty to Passionate Entrepreneur

MYRA EVANS-MANYWEATHER

COPYRIGHT © 2016 MYRA EVANS-MANYWEATHER
All rights reserved.

START WHERE YOU ARE
My Journey From Childhood Poverty to Passionate Entrepreneur

ISBN 978-1-61961-446-8 *Paperback*
 978-1-61961-447-5 *Ebook*

In loving memory of my father, Charles Evans, who gave me the courage to dream; my mother, Lula, who provided the nourishment for those dreams; my husband and son, Arthur and AC, who provided the inspiration; and my sisters, Sandra, Connie, and Regina, who kept me honest and held me accountable to start where I was planted—I thank God for giving me the best family for me.

CONTENTS

INTRODUCTION 9

Chapter One
COUSHATTA, LOUISIANA 17

Chapter Two
LIFE FROM THE OUTSIDE IN 33

Chapter Three
SIXTY MILES UP THE ROAD AND RISING 49

Chapter Four
AIMING HIGH 69

Chapter Five
BACK ON DUTY 83

Chapter Six
THE SOLUTION LIES WITHIN 105

Chapter Seven
WHAT IS YOUR OX-GOAD? 119

AFTERWORD 127

ACKNOWLEDGMENTS 129

ABOUT THE AUTHOR 131

INTRODUCTION

You Are Here

Have you ever seen one of those poster-sized maps they put up near the entrance to a large mall? Usually, it has a little red arrow on it with the words, "You are here."

I wish I'd had one the first time I saw Lackland Air Force Base. It's not until you leave San Antonio and see it from the highway that you realize just how big Lackland is. If you're somebody reporting for duty the first time, whatever you were expecting, it is much bigger than you thought it could be. Lackland is huge, as long and wide as the Texas plains. It's as big as life itself. Lackland is, in fact, the largest U.S. Air Force base in the world. When I first saw it back in 2002 after years of active duty in the Air Force, I was stunned. I had served on bases large and small, but Lackland was all by itself—vast and intimidating and a whole new size of large. But, in 2008, as I was returning after years of service in the US and overseas, Lackland had become extra-large, especially after merging Air Force, Army and Navy operations on the mega-base. It was like arriving in a strange and new city: I was immediately lost. I thought to myself, "This place is so big, *I don't even know where to start.*"

It took some doing, but I found my corner of the base and figured out where I was supposed to go. I worked in finance, keeping track of money, payroll, expenses, all of it. I started to settle in.

But in the course of establishing myself back at Lackland, I quickly learned that my responsibilities were too great for one person. I had to go out and hire someone to help. It was another lesson in learning how to start where I was, to step out of my fear and discover I could help myself by helping others.

So armed with a short list of potential candidates, I showed up at the desk of an Asian woman. Other than a very brief recommendation, I didn't know a whole lot about her. I found her sitting in another building, far away from where my office was. She was in a little space that couldn't even be called an office. She didn't even have a cubicle. She only had a desk—but she owned that space. It was the neatest little space that I'd ever seen. She was nervous—here was some strange retired officer wandering in out of the blue asking questions. But she more than managed, and in a few minutes, she was explaining in such great detail about the work that we do and how she goes about doing it. It was a better explanation than any I had heard in my twenty-some-year career. So I hired her. Her name is Ju Chen, though when I met her, she was going by Tammy. I learned so much from this woman! Of course, she tells the story a little bit differently; according to her it was all about how much *she* learned from *me*.

We sat and talked, and I couldn't help but notice how simple her space was. She had a computer on her desk. And that was it. But it was all she needed. She opened up one spreadsheet after another, and she walked me through a very detailed process, explaining how she tracked the major contracts within our organization. For example, we had the food service contract for the entire installation, the whole base. Lackland called itself the gateway to the Air Force, because every enlisted person entering the Air Force comes through Lackland. Food service was a massive $20 million contract. But this woman, sitting there in an open corner of an office, managed to track it all in such detail. She had it to the penny right there on her Excel spreadsheet. She had never even received any formal training; she had taught herself. And sitting right there she taught me how important it was to understand the mechanics—the process.

She understood what it meant to account for stuff and to be able to analyze data. Of course, I snapped her up. Over the next few weeks, I watched her closely: if a contract was out of balance, she would open another spreadsheet and pull out key information—the document number, the payment voucher, the receiving reports. She could get all of these pieces of information from one spreadsheet that drilled down into another. We have systems now for that, but she did it all manually, and she did it intuitively because she understood the process. It became obvious how wisely I had chosen. She'd be able to use the system that we had, not just to manage the contracts she was managing at that level, but soon she would do the same thing for the entire group. It was eight times the work, which she did with no additional stress.

And I learned something else. During our first review, I talked about how much she had helped the organization, and what we had accomplished together, and all that her work had meant. When I was done with that interview, I asked her if she had any questions. You know what her question was to me? She asked why I didn't say anything about her speech and how she spoke.

I said, "What do you mean?"

She said, "Do you understand what I'm saying?"

I said, "Yes, of course."

She told me that all of her career, her speech had limited her. All of her previous feedbacks had been about her accent, about how nobody could understand what she was saying. That had limited her, and she would never step out or speak up. She was intimidated, uncertain—just as I had been when I nervously stepped out of my office to look for help. And there she was. She told me she would never have asked for a promotion.

At the time, she was a technician, lower rung. She has now moved all the way up to the Headquarters Air Force level in the medical career resources field.

Many may ask why I begin my book with this story. The reason I tell this story is because the pair of us met and started where we were, and by working together and helping each other, we really achieved something. I was reminded of something I had learned when I was younger but had forgotten in the move to Lackland: I could rise above my anxieties and become an instrument of change for myself, for my family, for others. That has become my mission and my mantra: to be an instrument of change. By doing that, I can help others—by just listening carefully and helping them follow the path of their demonstrated competency, and by encouraging someone like Ju Chen to embrace her dreams. When we met and I asked about what she wanted to accomplish and what she wanted in her career, she told me—and all I had to do was encourage her to build on those things. Look where she is now.

Over the years, I've learned her story is even more inspiring. She's Taiwanese. She brought her family here one by one. She went back and got each one of them. She taught herself English here. She learned how to become a citizen of the United States. She delivered her family from abuse, poverty, from so many things. It's unbelievable.

By listening closely and helping somebody start *where they are*, you help them overcome adversity and use what they have learned along the way to do what they can and make a difference. And by doing that, you may find that you not only have helped them, you've helped yourself—and the organization you work for. Look what she's doing for the Air Force. And though we no longer work in the same office, I still count on her and go to her for advice about my personal finances. I have a degree in accounting, but she's the finance and tax person. She's done the books. She's done payroll. She's done it all. And she has only a high school degree. And she was worried about her accent!

This book begins with the story of Ju Chen, because all she needed to know was *how to start*. As I wrote above, by listening closely and helping somebody start *where they are*, you help them overcome adversity and use what they have learned along the way to do what they can and make a difference. Even people who are already accomplished and successful need to know where they are and how to get to where they want to go next.

That's why I wrote this book. *It's a book about how the only thing that's separating you from personal progress and success is knowing how to start where you are, use what you have, and do what you can…God will do the rest.* That idea has made a big difference in my life. I hope it will make a big difference to you, too.

CHAPTER ONE

COUSHATTA, LOUISIANA

Where I Started!

Some people are afraid of heights. Some people worry about the dark. We all fear something. I was afraid of the outhouse.

When I was growing up, the outhouse for me represented all that poverty was. It was so terrifying. I never wanted to go there. To me it was the darkest, ugliest, most fearful place of all. It was far from our little house, way out somewhere behind my grandmother's house; it had weeds all around it, and it was *not* somewhere I wanted to be. That outhouse was everything I knew I did not want in my life. I think you can find a figurative outhouse almost anywhere: even in your struggles, you have this ugliness, this craziness, this fear. You have to work to get past that, and for me that outhouse was the thing I had to get past.

I came from the unknown town of Coushatta, Louisiana, with nothing. That's where I started. Where I am today is a testament to my God, in whom all things are possible. It's a testament to my family, who wanted more for me than they had, and a testament to my belief that you can always start where you are and rise from there. I believe that anybody can be somebody.

You just have to take what you have and make what you want, and that comes from where you are. That sentiment was all around me as a child, whether I was washing dishes or washing down paper cardboard walls—because that's what our walls were made out of.

To make rooms, Dad had nailed cardboard to the wall framing. He would get old cartons from stores when they brought stuff in boxes. We broke down the cardboard, and we were excited when we got new cardboard to go on the walls, because of the water stains on the old pieces, but even though they were new, we had to wash those down. They had to be clean.

We had some old, brown carpet on the living room floor. I don't remember where it came from, but there was no such thing as a vacuum. *We* were the vacuum, and we had to sweep and sweep and sweep that carpet. It always seemed like there was a lot of dirt in it, and we had to clean that because you just walked into the living room through the door from outside. I remember when we got that carpet it seemed like we were moving up in the world. But when you live in the country, have no running water and only a human for a vacuum, you learn that hardwood floors, outhouses, and cardboard walls are not about poverty; it's about starting where you are and using what you have to survive and build.

When you start you will find your purpose along the way. My mission statement is "To be an instrument of change for my family, for my community and beyond." That's the mission, to be an instrument of change for whomever I touch. That might sound sophisticated but I didn't always know my purpose. My mantra has evolved from my high school valedictorian speech about how anybody can be somebody. I meant myself! I didn't know anything about mantras then; I didn't know anything about life mission statements. But as I go back and reflect over my life, I was implementing those things, I was doing those things and I know it came through education and training and the wisdom that comes from God.

I graduated from high school in 1981. We did have running water by then, but in 1976, before I went to high school, we didn't, and it seemed like it took forever to get it. They did not even run water down to the area where we were living, because we were on my grandmother's property. We were in what was supposed to be a storage shed. My grandmother had cows and pigs and chickens, and you had to store their feed and supplies, that's what this little shed of ours was really built for. We lived there because when my grandfather died, my mother decided to move to my grandmother's farm. We first lived with my grandmother in her house but my mother wanted a place for her family which included her husband and three little girls. So Mom was actually glad when my grandmother agreed that we could move into this storage shed! My Dad went out there and fixed it up, walled it up some more, and made some partitions and panels to divide it up and make three distinct rooms. In the beginning, we all slept in the same room, we three girls, my Mom and Dad. We put two beds in there and a pot-bellied stove. It was our furnace, right in the middle of the room. As a little girl, I thought it seemed way too far from my grandmother's house but was really only three or four hundred yards. But it was ours and it was home. At five everything seemed bigger anyway.

My grandmother didn't have running water either. She had a well, and so we had to draw our water. Our neighbor got running water before any of us, and so when they got running water, my Dad went into action. He was into net-

THE LIFE OF A MIDDLE CHILD

I'm sure you've heard the stories or read the stories about growing up in the middle. Well, I experienced all of those, but I didn't know anything about the middle-child syndrome itself. One of my sisters recently reminded me, because when I told them I was pursuing this book idea, I wanted to have a conversation with each of them to get their feelings on it.

My older sister isn't much of a diplomat. She basically said, "Myra, you were just annoying." That was her terminology for it. When I later spoke to her about some of my experiences, she said, "Have you ever read anything about the middle-child syndrome? There was nothing but that. You were just in the middle, so you were just annoying."

My baby sister said nothing bothered her because she was the baby, and so she had the benefit of both of us, so she said life was perfect for her. My older sister, interestingly enough, is only one year and a day older than I am. We both were born in July. She was born on the 25th, I was born on the 26th. My older sister was not even walking when I was born, and my Mom tells this story about how she used to carry both of us, one on each hip. She needed my sister to walk, but when my sister tells the story it's always different.

She said, "You always needed attention." She's talking from when she was still a baby and how Mom used to put us on her lap. She would lay her head on my Mom's lap and my Mom would just rub her head, because she had to take care of me.

The things that they did to me! I brought this up to them because I told them I probably would be sharing things like how they locked me in the closet, and how they used to tease me all the time. I told my Mom, "Mom, I really wasn't doing all this stuff," but in my house growing up, if one of you got in trouble you all got in trouble, which meant my older sister and I, we always got a whipping, even though I never did that bad stuff. But what I learned is sometimes your best just isn't good enough.

working before anybody knew what networking meant. I remember when we got our first family car. Dad became the "taxi driver" for many he knew. He knew *everybody*. My Dad was the only taxi driver in Coushatta, population 2,000. The issue with this taxi, he ran his taxi like a charity. He drove everybody everywhere at no charge, and he knew everybody in town. Of course I didn't understand that when I was little, so I hated to go anywhere with my Dad, because we always had to stop and talk to everybody on the street. I didn't realize it at the time, of course, but what he was doing was getting us out of that outhouse! The truth is, you can't help yourself until you have helped others. And if you really want to rise above, you must be willing to do what others won't, so you can have what others don't. It wasn't about my Dad; it was about his girls.

So Where Is Coushatta?

Coushatta is the parish seat of Red River. It is in northern Louisiana, in the northwestern quarter of the state, south of Shreveport, about thirty miles from Natchitoches, maybe three hours or more from New Orleans. When I would tell people I met in the military that I was from Louisiana, they would immediately assume I was from New Orleans and say, "Hey, you're from Louisiana. How's that gumbo?" But in reality the northern part of Louisiana is like being in a different state. I didn't eat gumbo;

I didn't even know what gumbo was made out of until I went to college. Gumbo's not like anything we had to eat...or at least that's not what we called the leftovers we mixed together for another meal. Actually, it's completely different, and I was always trying to explain that to people, too. I was always trying to explain one thing or another about growing up in Red River Parish. I would end up telling people, "Well, you know about Shreveport," because saying "Coushatta"—that didn't help them, not at all.

When I started middle school, I didn't think Coushatta was even on a map, but that was before I met a very great history teacher. I'll never forget old Mrs. Hite—there were two Ms. Hites, mother and daughter. They were both very good teachers. We called the mother "old" Mrs. Hite and the young one Miss Hite to distinguish them. As I was saying, Mrs. Hite knew history. She taught *real* Louisiana history and so we knew things, such as Louisiana was special because only Louisiana still had parishes. Other states had counties, but we had parishes, and Coushatta was important, because it's the parish seat of Red River Parish. We had a courthouse, and so we were somebody. The more I learned, the more important my hometown became to me. When you start where you are because that's where you are, and you make a point to learn all you can about that place, you are bound to find some good in it that you can use to do better...God will do the rest.

The View Out the Bus Window

We lived outside Coushatta, on the same road as Edgefield. Edgefield was an all-white community with maybe 200 people living in it. I'll never forget the route when we were being bused to Coushatta School. We would get on the bus, and then we would drive to Edgefield to pick up the kids there. The bus made this loop around the village, and I would look out the window at all the nice, beautiful homes. Then the whites would get on the bus. They picked us up first—the little cluster of old houses and sheds where we lived didn't have a name. But every time those white kids would get on the bus, I'd think, "Thank God we get picked up first," so nobody could see where we were from. Only relatives got on the bus out where I lived.

There were a lot of class divisions in Coushatta, and you could see them all from the windows of the bus. They were especially apparent when the bus went up a road like Ashland Road, and you'd pass through different communities along the way. In the first part of Ashland Road, there was a friend of ours, just somebody we saw around, but when I finally found out where that friend lived, I was shocked. I thought *I* was poor! I saw that there were families even worse off than mine, and this kid was from one. They just lived out in some field, as far as I could tell.

It was weird, too, since most of the other houses on that

road were nice homes. Today, the whites have all moved out and there are a lot of blacks living in that area now. You can tell the difference, but in that neighborhood when I was younger, there were certain places you just didn't go. I still remember going across the Red River, which flowed out of the plains, down into Louisiana, past Coushatta and south toward Alexandria and the Gulf. We'd cross the river just outside town where you could see an old "for-colored" bathroom and water fountain. It was still there in my time; it freaked me out. I was born in 1963, so by the early 1970s, when I started going to school, it was one of the leftovers from the old days; not that people were still using it, but it was there, and it had those words on it. I remember seeing it and how it made me feel.

It hammered home for me that there are people who might not think I'm somebody special just because my family says so. The bathroom and fountain have been torn down by now, but I remember passing them when we started having to go across the river to pick up students for Springville Junior High.

The black community in Coushatta was concentrated in a couple of areas, downtown and across the river in Hanna and Grand Bayou. My family was much closer to the Martin area, northeast of town. We weren't considered town people, and of course that made me feel like a poor, country girl. I thought that the blacks who lived in town were probably richer than us because—well, because they lived in town. I thought that if you lived in town, you had running water. I found out later that that was not the case. It doesn't matter where you are from; what matters is where you are going, and I was going away from Coushatta one day.

Integration Comes to Coushatta?

Integration was not quick to arrive in my hometown. That part of the south was segregated for most of my early school years. In elementary school and through the beginning of my high school years, a lot of blacks went to their school and the whites went to their school. There was *Brown v. Board of Education* in 1954, and we got the Civil Rights Act in 1964, but in Red River Parish, we still had pockets of segregation in 1974. That all changed in my junior year of high school with "forced integration"—a mandatory busing order to comply with the Justice Department court order to desegregate Red River Parish.

There was so much confusion on both sides, because each wanted their school to stay open. Not all black families thought much of the idea of integrating, either. Local black leaders were telling us not to go, to boycott. We were segregated in my elementary years for sure. In

Coushatta, the black school became the public school for grades 5 through 8, and white Coushatta High became the school for all of the public high school students. Right after segregation, the private Riverdale Academy opened in 1970. Their team name is "The Rebels"—what does that tell you? Today, it's still a private school, and the team is still called "The Rebels" And there was a public school out in Martin, out past where we lived; it was public, but only whites went there, so really we were not forced to integrate until my junior year. Most of us decided to stay separate, so even though the law said there was no more segregation, the school system in Red River Parish was not really integrated until my junior year.

Before desegregation I did get to know some of the white kids, but in unexpected, sometimes tragic ways. For example, we lived just off the highway—Highway 7—right across the street from a country church. One day, when I was still a little girl, there was an accident: it involved a carload of people, an entire family, a white family. I believe one of them was killed.

We were home when it happened, so of course we all went running to see if we could help. I remember my Mom went out to help first, and then my grandmother. Then they came running back to get something to help with all the bleeding. I was little, but I remember how surprised I was when they came running back out of the house with the white towels. They always believed in having white towels. We didn't use them; I thought they were just for show. But you always *had* to have white towels. Seeing Mom and Big Mama come out with all those new white towels and using them to try to stop the bleeding of this family—I mean it was a mess, and the white towels found their purpose in my mind. It was another reminder to use what you have in your hands.

As it happened, that family lived in Edgefield and, years later, we all ended up riding the bus together. Some of them knew that that's where they had had the accident, and they knew we had helped the best we could. It really impressed me seeing how my family came to the rescue. I know they thanked my grandmother. But that experience really hit me. I knew my family had helped this white family, and it was almost like a bond of some kind was formed. It was a powerful experience.

Those days were very chaotic and very stressful, but all of those events and people influenced me growing up even though I didn't understand it all. During that accident, I asked myself, "Now, why are we doing this?"

I was always confronted with things that my Mom and my family did for others. My mom would always say, "You help no matter what the situation is, no matter what the color and all of that."

It made me question, though, would the same thing have happened if it were a black family having an accident in an all-white neighborhood? Because getting bused to an all-white high school was tough. All the divisions in the town were on display, with people talking about boycotts and all that. Can you imagine? They wanted kids *not* to go to school. They, no kidding, asked us *not to go*. It was not just white resistance. It was the black leaders in the town who asked us not to go to the white public school—it was the pastors, it was our schoolteachers, it was those black people who lived in the town and who would serve on the council. Everyone was fighting for their "kind," or so they thought. I was hopeful that the situation would improve after full integration, because we had heard all these rumors about them having better books and better opportunities, and that they did better in school. So by the time the school year started, I was very hopeful that things would look up. I was excited about something new. But there was a price to pay.

I had started ninth grade at Coushatta High School, which is called Red River High now, but I graduated from Martin High School, home of the Red Devils—another interesting name for a school. It was run like a private school. Until a couple of us black students showed up, only white kids went there; it mostly catered to the Martin community, and in those days Martin was all white. I became the first black to graduate there with honors.

There was nothing that said that we *couldn't* go there, but nobody went there—nobody black, that is except maybe one. But in 1979 when they forced integration and provided buses to get us there—well, then that's where we went. That was a very difficult thing to do, because everybody was running around telling my Mom and the other black parents to boycott, boycott school! And a lot of the other black families went along with it and did not send their kids to school on that first day. I could have said, like many of them said, "I'm not going to that school. That's helping the white man. I'm not going to go. I'm going to stay here. Whatever." But no, I made a choice that I'm going to go, because who would I be hurting by not going? Besides, my mother was not having it.

It wasn't going to hurt the white man if I didn't go. I'd be hurting myself because the new school had books. They had newer books, labs, and a big library. They had a whole lot more things, so I thought anyway.

My mother, Lula, was not impressed by others' arguments: "You're going to be at school on day one!" So I went to school. It felt as if I were leaving all my friends, because most of the people I knew were going to the old school. In fact, my older sister, the one who is a year older than me, got a chance to graduate from Coushatta High School. That was her senior year, and many of them had already ordered class rings and so she got a chance to stay.

First Day at a New School

As juniors, we *had* to go to the new school, and so I went. I wanted to embrace it. If I was told I couldn't do something, or if I was told something was going to be too difficult, I wanted to prove otherwise. That's how I felt, so off I went—and the first day was everybody checking everybody out. I thought that was weird. What could be so scary about being around someone who didn't look like you?

There were only a handful of us blacks. So people I barely spoke to from Coushatta High—all of a sudden, we kind of clung together because we were all in the same boat. But I'll be honest with you, and I don't think I've ever said this before: *I wanted to be different.* I did not want to hang around just with people that looked like me, because I didn't think that was going to get me very far.

Of course I got teased about that, too, because now, to the other kids, I became the butt-kisser to the white man.

I'm not dark, that is, my skin color is not dark black, and there's a saying: "Among the minorities, there are minorities within the minorities." I felt that was true, because I was lighter than most all of the other blacks who were there. And they thought I was getting preferential treatment! So it was very stressful, because people don't want to be identified by their race, their color, or any of those things. Nobody does. *Nobody.* Yet, there I was. That was the craziest thing for me. One positive thing that came out of it was learning to excel despite my differences and embracing everybody as somebody.

CHAPTER TWO

LIFE FROM THE OUTSIDE IN

One day, I was talking to my mother about some of the problems I was facing at school. I didn't want to be known as somebody trying to get ahead by "butt-kissing" anybody. I told her what was going on, but she stopped me. She said, "Myra, people are jealous."

I said, "Mom, you give that answer to everything. Why would people be jealous of me? I don't have anything."

But my mother knew more than I'll ever know, especially about reading people: People's jealousy didn't have to be about what you really *had*, it could be about what they *thought* you had. I had something much greater, something that others may not have had: I knew I was loved by my family. I had that, and many didn't.

The high school in Martin was a small school. There were only sixteen of us in my class—and I was the outsider. Thirteen kids who grew up together, played together, shared secrets together. And me and two other blacks who joined them in 1979. So there was controversy when I was appointed the class valedictorian. The other families did not want that to happen. One family especially did not want that to happen—the parents of a white girl who had been there for four years. She had become a friend of mine but I knew she felt that seniority mattered, and she felt she deserved it because she had been there four years and I had not. But in the end our grade point averages were just too far apart. They couldn't justify it. I had a very high GPA—and she wasn't close.

There were other tense moments while I was at Martin. The principal there took a lot of heat, because when they opened up a work-study program at the school, he picked me to work in the secretary's office. He called me in. He had some great words of encouragement; he said he saw things in me that he was pleased with. He took a chance, and it worked out. I was the first black they had working in the office and I was worried about how I would get along with the secretary, an older white lady. But she and I got along really well, and she always liked it when I was working. She said things like, "Oh those kids play too much." And me, I was serious—probably *too* serious. I followed rules. I followed instructions, and I *always* reported to her when I needed to be out or if something came up and I wasn't able to work.

She said I treated it more like a real job. She was right. My Mom wouldn't have had it any other way. It was my first significant job one with responsibilities and a real boss. It was a start.

Seeing Is Believing

Some people come to these kinds of realizations through faith, but I am very literal. I need to have things shown to me. I'm not without faith, of course. I have the attitude of "This is all about God," but way back then, when I sat in church on the mourning bench—that's where they put you in this little church when you said you were ready to accept Jesus Christ as your Savior—I stayed on it the whole week and never came up. The pastor was preaching to me about how my hands were going to change, and my feet would look new and all that stuff. And me, I was waiting for that to happen.

I took things way too literally, especially all that preaching, and so my Mom had to sit down with me and ask me why I hadn't come off the bench.

"Mom," I said, "Look at my feet. Look at my hands. Nothing has changed." I would be praying, praying, praying, when the preacher was there. I'd be down there on my knees, and I would sneak and look at my hands. I was looking for those hands to look new, and they didn't!

Fortunately, God put people in my life to explain the biblical metaphors and secrets. I remember the Sunday school teacher, whom we called Cousin Lucy but whose exact relationship to me was unclear until years later, and who tried to explain to me really what it was all about, and I started to cry, saying, "Well, yeah, I believe in God. But *what about my new feet?!*" I was so literal. I didn't truly understand it until much, much later. But when I came out of the water, I was shouting...just like the others.

I later confessed to Mom, and everybody, that the day I said I accepted Christ, I didn't truly understand what all that meant. I knew what I had heard, but I had taken it all so literally. That's why, to this day, I'm so against a literal interpretation of the Bible, or a literal interpretation of anything, because I know how much damage it can do to people.

For me, faith is truly about the *application*. Can I *apply* what I read in the Bible to my situation today? That's where I get my peace, and my calm, and my ability to navigate the different things that I have to go through. I have to be able to apply it.

I think the application of the Word is where wisdom is gained, and we don't do it individually; we do it with others, collectively. We collaborate, and we come together, and we have discussions, and we begin to learn from each other. God created us for community, and if we don't thrive in a community, then we're limiting ourselves, and we're limiting God's ability to use us to our full potential. That's why I believe we start where we are, do what we can, and let God do the rest.

Taking the Plunge

Junior and senior years were my two years at the new high school. My life changed along with the times. I joined the cheerleader squad. It was, of course, an all-white team of girls. I was the only black. I never really could get into cheerleading before. Not only did it get me out of my comfort zone, it got me into something that I really hadn't given a lot of thought to. I went to the football games and the basketball games. I ended up enjoying being there and supporting the teams.

Initially I think *everybody* was uncomfortable with my being a cheerleader. They were uncomfortable with it, and I was uncomfortable with it. But it turned out to be a great experience. One of the girls and I really became friends. Her mother would host the practices at their home. I would be included in the things the others did. It was very important, and it made me face some obstacles I hadn't anticipated. For example, the cheerleader tried to teach me to swim—but I'm *still* afraid of water. Before I turned fifty, I took a swim class because I said, "I am going to do this." And I did. Now I'm able to go across the pool, with a floaty of course. I still don't consider myself a swimmer, but at least I got over the fear of water.

During that time, I did actually get in the pool with them. I didn't know any black people who could swim. We did not have a pool to go to. Everybody who swam that *I* knew just swam in the lake. Swimming pools weren't something that I had been exposed to. So I got in the water with them. I jumped in! The lady tried to teach me to swim, and it was fun, but I was afraid of the water and I must admit, there were some trust factors too, so I didn't make much progress.

I could never get used to the water around my ears. And as a young black girl, having to have her hair straightened every week, I didn't dare get my head in the water because my hair would "nap up" and 'I'd have to do it again. There was a pool in Coushatta, or so I'm told. I think it was just like the movie theater—closed to coloreds back then.

Change Comes to Coushatta

When we integrated, they closed the movie theater completely. We weren't allowed to go to it anyway. My Mom said that when she was growing up, if you went, you had to sit up in the top balcony with the other black people. But by the time I came of age, there was no movie theater in Coushatta to go to. It sat on the corner for years and years, and they closed it down right at integration. They just weren't going to have it. It's like they were saying, "You just weren't going to be integrated." We lived with this building on the corner in Coushatta for years. It was empty and stayed that way. It seemed like an angry thing. They weren't going to make it useful. They weren't going to make it into a community center or anything like that. It was almost as if the town said, "Okay, integration is here to stay. We got to do it. But we don't have to play the game; we don't have to do it as part of our community life." They finally tore the old building down, and I never got to step one foot inside it.

During all this, there was a lot of whispering and stuff that we didn't understand. There was this feeling that this is the way it is and you have to accept that. My mom and dad were very passive about all this. They kind of just accepted things the way they were and they did not push beyond that. My grandmother had been in the city for a long time. In fact, my grandmother babysat the man who later became the district attorney. She was like his "nanny," so to speak. He had a lot of respect for my grandmother, and we liked him. We accepted that there were just some good whites. There were also some that weren't so good, but we had to stay in our place, so to speak. Or that's how I felt—that that's how things were. You don't go and try to force yourself into the swimming pool, for example. We were just told not to go. We didn't go to those places because we were very obedient in those days; a parent's rule was law.

Cheerleading, on the other hand, leveled the playing field, at least for me. I learned that the other girls were no different from me. They liked to have fun. They enjoyed cheerleading, and I felt confident around them. I could have feared them, I guess, but I didn't feel deprived or that I was poor when I was with them. It's a cliché, but I felt like they put their clothes on the same way I put on mine. That was my big take-away: If you set aside your fears and prejudices and allowed yourself to get to know people, you'd find there were good ones and there were bad ones.

When I was out on a basketball court and cheerleading, it's a fun place. I found out just how much fun. I wasn't somebody who really liked to have *fun*, I would say. As I mentioned, I was serious by inclination. But by allowing

JUDY W.

Not everybody on the squad was open and friendly, but some were, and Judy Walker especially so, at least in my eyes. She was very friendly, very outgoing. She didn't seem to see me as a black person or see herself as a white person. Not once did I ever hear her make even a small remark about any differences between us.

Judy had long, brown hair. And she wasn't thin, which at the time I thought was another good thing. Judy was a normal person, while most of the cheerleaders were blonde and real little. But I think the main thing about Judy was that she opened the door: It's like that old formula, if you want to be in with a certain crowd, you have to find someone who is not only *in* but also different. She was that person for me.

She allowed me to be there, because if I showed up and there was nobody else to talk to, I could always count on being able to have a conversation with Judy. She accepted me. I was never standing by myself. I was never the outsider and never had to feel like an outsider. She would always insist that I be brought into the conversation. I'll never forget her. I didn't have a car, and there were many times I wouldn't have been able to get to practice, or if I did get there, I didn't have a ride home. But without fail, Judy and her brother would bring me home or come to pick me up to make sure I got to practice.

Judy helped me see that there are good people everywhere, in every race, in every culture. There are just some really good people out there. The trick is finding them. Judy found me.

---

myself to go to those games, by committing to shared excellence, I blocked everything else out. When you do that, you find out that you can be together, on the same side, on the same team. That was the good thing about me choosing to get involved. By participating in a sport or being on the cheerleader team, I was in. I wanted everyone to see that they could be in, too.

Everybody liked a basketball game regardless of who was playing. And when we came out on the basketball court we were all on the same team, cheering for the same people. I never heard any racist stuff. And I wasn't the world's greatest acrobat, so of course I couldn't do all of the twists and turns that my counterparts did. That didn't seem to bother them or me. I played a supporting role, and I played it very well. Nobody complained. I just got started, did what I could, and trusted God to do the rest.

Graduation Day

For me, for any student, being the class valedictorian is quite an achievement. And for any valedictorian, the crowning moment is The Speech, the moment when you are asked to stand up in front of your peers and represent the brightest among them.

I remember my speech to this day. I wanted to leave a mark. I was aware that I was the first one; that I was different, that I had succeeded. I was aware that giving that speech was an opportunity I had earned and that I couldn't take it lightly.

I did not want to leave anyone with the thought that I got it because I was black or anything like that. I wanted to be able to use that moment to make sure others would be able to gain from it. I took it very seriously. I did research. I went to the library. I took a lot of time writing the speech. There was one quote that I distinctly remember putting in there, one that really meant something to me. It was a message to everyone, and it was, "Anybody can be somebody. Take what you have and make what you want. It can be done. It has been done." That was my message.

It was a small school with a big, full ceremony. After the graduation we formed a receiving line, and I was standing there with my gold valedictorian's cord around my neck. This white man came up to me, shook my hand, and said, "You must have earned it, because they wouldn't have given it to you otherwise."

I was taken aback. He was sincere, and it made me very happy. It helped me understand that my effort could be appreciated for what it was. That comment lifted me. I knew that when the going got tough, we would all come together, and that I had something inside of me that I didn't recognize at that time. It took a stranger to point it out to me.

My speech was well received. I actually got a standing

ovation. My mother and father were there, and of course they were proud. It was a proud moment regardless of the fact that it was a small graduating class. My parents were there, too, when that white man came up to me and gave me that compliment: "You must have earned it."

Because let me tell you, the one thing I hated most while I was there: For each of the two years I was there, every year we had to have a "black-every-award" category. We had to have one black prizewinner and one white one. It was a small class! But the only category that didn't have to have that was class valedictorian. They didn't have a black Valedictorian and a white Valedictorian. They had me.

The Card

When I graduated, my father handed me a little card. I opened it. It said, "As you go through life, remember you're equal to any man." It wasn't frilly or in any respect the *girl card*. I cried. That card is with me today. I talked about that card in my retirement ceremony when I left the Air Force.

Looking back on it now, for me what that card said was, *as you go through life, remember there is nothing you can't do because of the color of your skin*. It spoke to me in so many ways later in life. I would reflect on that card after my dad

died and know that he loved me so much more than I ever could have imagined. And my proof was there in that card.

My dad died in 1989. He wasn't there to see me go through my career at the Air Force. But oh my goodness, that card was with me everywhere. My dad had his share of problems. He obviously drank too much—and I still have issues with people that drink—but I know my dad loved us. He was *there*, he didn't leave, and in his own way he gave me a legacy that is so, so powerful. I did not let my skin color or my sex determine where I was going to go in any situation.

When you see someone else that's doing something and they say you can't do it? That's a motivator within itself. When they were telling me that I couldn't go to this school and be successful, I was determined to show that not only was I not getting any special treatment, but I was going to succeed, too. What I had was who I was, and I could be just as good there as I had been before. And I had the card to prove it.

Two Teachers

I think most people have one or two teachers in their formal education who really shape them as people. I was lucky enough to find two truly amazing women in that little high school in Martin. Both taught me valuable lessons that extended far beyond the classroom.

Miss Sibley was one. She really inspired me. She was a black lady. When I was in her class I would always make As. Always. But on papers and exams, I always missed one or two key points or questions, which hurt my grades even though I was often the first one to finish. She called me in one day and said, "Myra, why do you think you always miss one or two on these English exercises?" She wanted to know if I had a rationale for making my choices.

I told her, "When I miss one, it's because to me it sounded

right or it sounded wrong." I was in my junior year at a new school, but it took Miss Sibley to tell me for the very first time how to distinguish between the singular and plural forms of a simple verb; she taught me that what she called "a plural verb"—like "they ran," for example—did not have an S, but a "singular" verb—"he runs"—did. After that, my grades were perfect. It was something that simple. She recognized that I had natural talent. Everybody needs somebody to point out the one little thing that can help them build upon what they have.

She represented that for me, something that simple that has stayed with me. She helped me to understand that I could go to school, get college work-study or get other kinds of financial support, that I could apply for grants. What a difference that made!

The other black teacher who really helped shape me was Mrs. McDuffy. She was a ball of fire. I hated history, absolutely hated history. But this history teacher made the subject come alive in the classroom. When she taught American history we *saw* the Boston Tea Party. You could really see it, hear it—you could see the tea being thrown into the harbor. When she talked about slavery, you felt the pain, the suffering, the humiliation. And she brought to the classroom stories about black people who had invented important things, useful things, history-changing things.

I thought, "Yes, there are people like me who have succeeded and made a difference." Through Mrs. McDuffy's and Miss Sibley's teaching, I was able to reshape some of my thinking about who we were as a people—black people. It was okay for me to want to make a difference, to contribute, to find my own way of contributing, and to encourage others to do the same and to find another starting place, a way to move forward in a new direction.

CHAPTER THREE

SIXTY MILES UP THE ROAD AND RISING

When I think back about how my life has been changed just by listening carefully when people I admired spoke to me, I'll always remember Miss Sibley's little talk to me the day after I gave my valedictorian speech. Her private speech may have made a bigger impact on me than my own very public speech.

I had finally, and officially, graduated from high school and, maybe unlike many kids my age, I felt like I had a responsibility to start earning money right away so I could help take care of the family. I was thinking that if I went to college, I'd have to wait four years before I'd be able to earn enough money to be able to help anybody. I explored a local vo-tech with an administrative program: nine months at that school and I would have a job and I would be able to pay a light bill—pay two or three light bills. Even a water bill! I was sorely tempted.

Miss Sibley's Last Lesson for Me

Thank God for Miss Sibley. When she heard I was thinking of not going to college, she asked me to stop by her office. I did, and as we talked over my plan, I thought she would approve of my eagerness to start earning a living and encourage me. Miss Sibley listened to my vo-tech dream, and, surprisingly, said, "Oh, no-no-*no*, Myra, that would be such a waste. That's a mistake."

I was startled by her insistence. She patiently helped me understand that I could go to school, get college work-study, or get other kinds of financial support. I could apply for grants and all of those things. What a difference that made.

So, I underwent a sudden change of plans. I didn't know where to apply. Grambling was near me, and my sister was there, but in Coushatta, everyone said, "Nothing good comes out of Grambling." But I knew better, my oldest sister was already there, and she was super smart! My band director also had graduated from there and he taught me the value of diversity through the universal language—music.

There was a white college next door to Grambling, a big, well-known university: LSU. And there was a mixed, but mostly white, school down the road about thirty miles called NSU, Northwestern State University. Some people told me go there. But I said no, if I was going to go, I was going to go to a black university because they needed good people. If I was as good as Miss Sibley said, then I would be able to succeed there—and maybe then people would be able to say that something good came out of Grambling.

So I started researching my options, and I found a financial aid grant. I didn't get a scholarship because I didn't know about applying for one. I did get a small "scholarship" from my church—more like a gift really. It was about $100. I didn't have anyone sitting down with me explaining to me that there were hundreds and hundreds of scholarships out there that I could have applied for. But my band teacher finished at Grambling, and he actually helped us fill out the grant papers.

The first year, I had to stay in the freshman dorm; it was a rule. After that my sister and I shared a room. I looked up to her and thought the world of her. But I remembered that on her first day at Grambling, she cried. She called home and got Mom all upset. She was complaining that she had to stand in long, long lines and when she'd finally get her turn, they'd tell her she wasn't in the right place, and she'd have to start over. She didn't have enough money. She was just falling apart and I remember thinking, when I get there, I won't call home about the lines being too long.

So I made a game out of it. When I called home my first day from college, I was *happy*. I played hopscotch. I hopped from one line to the other. One thing I'm not going to do, I promised myself: I'm not going to call home crying. My mom didn't want me to go in the first place. Two of us in college, and nobody helping at home—or so I thought. But nothing was further from the truth. My mom knew how hard it would be if we didn't get an education. She wanted more for her girls—all of us.

Dark Days

Looking back, I probably should have gone somewhere else—or just stayed in Coushatta. I just didn't feel ready for all that responsibility. I'd go from an *Aha*-moment to a very, very low moment, where I would just cry, cry, cry. I would think about this tree in our backyard. When I was younger, I'd go and hide behind that tree and cry. I never felt like I belonged, and I needed to feel that I did. When I was younger, I didn't feel like I was respected or that I got any approval. My sister said that I required too much approval, but all I knew was I just always felt depressed. As I was growing up there was so much poverty around me. I used to think, "How can anybody be happy living like this?"

As a child my pleasures were few. I loved playing jacks with my mom and dad. I would love that. We'd all be sitting around on the floor playing jacks. I remember when we taught Mom how to play Uno when Uno first came out. We'd laugh and we'd have a good time. But growing up, in those early years, there just weren't enough of those good times and laughter.

I used to write a lot of poems about how I really felt—and they were ugly. Not the poems, the feelings. But by the time I went to Grambling, I knew I didn't want to hurt my parents. I knew they loved me. I did not understand why I felt so low. Sometimes, I'd go back to Coushatta during my time at Grambling, and I would see myself staring out the bus window again. I would stare out at the passing countryside and think of how I wished things were different.

Some of the adults who paid me attention hurt me, because some of the attention was not appropriate. I understood it was not appropriate, but I was very young, and I can't say that I did not want the attention. Sometimes, when you're a kid, you feel any attention is better than no attention. But I was a child. I knew you could be book smart, but not have all the common sense that you needed because you're still growing and maturing. With all the grown-up attention, I felt so much more mature than my counterparts, my peers. I'd tell myself that was why they were reaching out to me. They felt they could talk to *me*. I could have real intellectual conversations. That's what I told myself, even when I knew what was happening wasn't right. I was never raped or anything like that, but I was not treated like the child I was. And then, when I found out that I wasn't the only one, that other girls were also having those "real intellectual conversations" too. I was crushed, absolutely crushed.

I needed to believe I was good in everything I did. I mean, I poured my heart into it. But I believed that my peers hated me. Remember, high school was two different schools for me. I never felt like I got along with my peers. At my first high school—and from elementary school through junior high—it was hate. What else would you call it? My band boots were taken from my locker and sliced up; three young black boys held me down in the gym; and my face was scratched up in a fight that wasn't mine! Yes, I felt hated.

My depression was serious but I didn't treat it as such. Often I beat myself up saying, if I was really a Christian, surely, I wouldn't be this sad. But I thank God for doctors and for medication, because once I retired from the Air Force and got on a cycle with the medication, I honestly was able to see clearly and know for sure where I wanted to go. Before it was like a roller coaster. One day I had these high, high, highs—I was all over the place and wanted to do everything and was going, going, going. Then I would have these lows, and I could just say to myself, "Oh, woe is me." There was constant crying on my part, and I didn't understand where all that was coming from. At the same time, even though I was going through that, it was fueling me. Oh man, people would say I'd just go, go, go, and wanted to do, do, do, but I didn't know at the time, I didn't realize that the depression was driving me, but it was. Depression fueled by the fear of failure was driving me crazy.

Someone once said, "You've got to get sick and tired of being sick and tired in order to really change." When you get to that point in life, that's when things begin to change for you. As long as you're comfortable, you're going to keep doing the same thing you've always done and think you're going to get a different result. As they say, "That's insanity," and I agree. That's what I was doing: driving myself insane, making the same choices over and over again. I can see that so clearly now, whereas at sixteen, seventeen, eighteen, I just wanted more. I knew that, but I didn't have a plan on how to get there, and I didn't know what was missing. I needed a plan to get to the next chapter and little did I know then that I could get there just by starting where I was.

So I stumbled through my first two years of college. My sister was a big help and there were occasional teachers who would try to help me along. And I did become a little more social. I majored in accounting and I was a part of the business leaders' club and the school accounting club. We would invite business people down to speak to us about what it was like being an accountant. It sounded like something that people were always telling me, that that's what I was going to become. But it didn't sound like Myra to me.

At Grambling, things slowly changed for me. I had started as a child who just wanted to be a grown-up. But as I socialized and got to know other people, I became a friendlier person myself. I started to enjoy my life. I liked the steppers, the music, and the fun. I enjoyed going to the football games, because we cheered. We embraced that. But when it came down to work, we worked hard, too. I learned that it was okay for me to smile. It was okay for me to have a good time. We played hard, but my expectation for myself and for others was to work just as hard. Yes, Grambling was the start of something beautiful, and it was right where I was.

What I Learned at Grambling

Grambling did a very good job of taking care of each of us as people, and instilling confidence in us as black people. Grambling had a lot of issues—and still does—but they were never indifferent. A vast majority of the administrators and the teachers really cared about their students. In fact—and this may make you laugh—but I remember one teacher who called me in because I had on a sundress, but I had never shaved. She told me that if I wore the sundress again that I needed to shave under my arms. That's part of a complete education. Where else would a teacher have done that? A Grambling education was about the whole person.

The main thing I took from Grambling was the belief that that there were good black people. There were smart black people too, and they were willing to help. The teacher who came to me and told me that I needed to shave was dealing with me not as a name on a class list, but as a whole young person who needed to learn.

From Grambling, I also took away the realization that even

as a leader you had to care about the whole person, not just one aspect and not just getting the right numbers. I learned how important leadership is, and the importance of integrity, the character that you have to have in order to be a successful leader. It was not about doing the least. In many cases, it was about doing the most—and not just for you but for others too. Leadership was a huge takeaway for me. The second thing I took away from Grambling was the discovery that women could be leaders. That potential was not just for the men. Up until that time, it seemed it would always be a man who was leading the detachment commanders, the cadet commanders, whatever.

The third thing I took away from Grambling came in the form of a lot of firsts. We had an astronaut, Guion Bluford, come and speak to us, and I was just in awe. There were a lot of firsts that I got to experience at Grambling. I realized that even in the military, they needed good people, and it was okay to go into the military. I learned that it was okay for smart people to enter the military.

And the fourth thing I learned at Grambling was starting where you are has no respect for color, creed, religion, or other. Everyone has to start where they are. Using what you have is a choice and a commandment. And doing what you can is a mandate and an obligation if you are to go to the next level.

A Woman in Uniform

One day toward the end of my sophomore year, I caught a glimpse of a woman in uniform coming down the sidewalk. She changed everything. I saw Colonel Rosetta Armour-Lightner walking across campus. She was a black lady. She was tall, dignified, with a huge presence. She had a beautiful smile; it just lit up everything. Even her walk was impressive—she carried herself with so much confidence. I still remember it: When I saw her coming, it was like she controlled that sidewalk. She was *there*. You knew she was *there*. She understood who she was—I couldn't imagine her thinking the same thoughts I was thinking about myself and my future. She seemed very powerful. At the time, I was dating this guy who was in ROTC; he had told me that a new commander was coming to Grambling. When I saw her, I thought, "I bet that's her. Wow, there are actually females in the military who are in control of stuff!" I was very, very impressed; I'll never forget what a great feeling it was.

I made my way over to the ROTC detachment and I spoke with an officer and a staff sergeant. I asked a few questions. I certainly didn't go there to join, but as I talked to them, they started explaining the possibility that I could join ROTC in the summer and get a big and unexpected benefit: "You'll have all your tuition paid." That took my breath away. Then the officer, Capt. Wright, added, almost apologetically, "and you'll be paid $100 a month, yours to do with what you want." Now *that* sounded exciting.

So before I knew it, I had agreed to take an entrance exam. I felt safe because I was always terrible at standardized exams. But surprisingly I scored very well in administration and, although this would have surprised people who knew me, in navigation. This was a big deal to the recruiters. They thought they had a unicorn—a black female who was interested in navigation. "This is huge," they said. "This is *great*." So they rushed me into a medical exam, where I found that one of the standards for being a navigator was you had to have a certain seating height. I'm not very tall. I was off by maybe an inch or two, but they were determined. It was going to require a waiver. I'll never forget the officer calling me in and saying, "Just how bad do you want to be a navigator?" I looked at him like he was speaking a foreign language. I said, "It's not that important to me, frankly," because I can't even find my way out of my garage—and I didn't even have a garage. I have no perception of north, right, left, south, east, or west. I said, "That would just be a disaster." He sighed, and we reverted to "administration." I had to write my essay for the scholarship, and of course I got it.

Once I earned the scholarship, they did what they promised and picked up my tuition. I was already getting a grant so that helped tremendously. Imagine: there's my mom with two girls in school, so the grant was very important. The tuition was even better, because now I would be able to have a little money left over to do other things. And I was in the college work-study program. So: I went to school, I worked, I got that scholarship, I got that grant—and because of all that, I left Grambling debt-free. Just think, if I'd never got started, I'd never have finished!

My sister didn't follow me into the military, but she had scholarships and she had her own college work-study, and she had grants. The important thing for my family was that neither one of us left Grambling owing money. There were six of us and we were living on less than $10,000 annual income, and now she has seen the two of us graduate with no student loans and no debt. Nothing but God.

That was huge. If we hadn't pulled that off, we would not have been able to afford anything else. For me, the ROTC scholarship wouldn't be there if I didn't keep my grades up. They weren't large scholarships, but they helped, and once you proved yourself at school, then you got scholarships from other sources, like the business department. If your grade point average was high enough in the business department—and my sister and I both were always one and two in accounting—they awarded scholarships. That hard work paid off. I hear today about the huge, huge debt that our kids are going into to get a college education. It's just mind-boggling, because one thing I've realized is that not everybody is cut out to go to a four-year college. All they're doing is getting deeper in debt. They're coming out, and they still are no more functional or able to find a job or able to contribute to society. They might have done just as well if they'd found a trade or explored something else they were interested in and could really do and enjoy doing.

I've had to rethink everything. During the Industrial Revolution, we needed people who had been mass-produced, so to speak. If you were one of them, you would go in and learn a set of rules and produce something. Some people enjoyed the factory and were happy producing something useful based on a checklist or whatever. Today, though, that is no longer the society in which we live. We have outsourced all of those types of jobs. So now what? If you're not being a doctor or a lawyer or something very specific like that what are you being trained to do? Our schools do not do a very good job of training people to problem solve and think for themselves, or be creative and make ways where there are no ways. So what are you waiting for? Get started where you are.

First Step Into the Wild, Blue Yonder

Finally, I graduated Summa Cum Laude with a 3.9 average. I was a very good student—near the top. That means a lot in ROTC. Most people in the program can't get a regular commission. When you graduate from one of the major academies, the Air Force Academy, the Naval Academy, and West Point, a regular commission is automatic because those are military schools and that's why they exist. But to earn a regular commission coming out of ROTC at a small state school is very rare. I earned a regular commission.

At first, I wanted to turn it down because I didn't understand it. I was thinking, "I'm not going into the military for a career. I'm going to get my master's and then I'm out of there." Sort of the same way I was thinking about high school and college; I didn't really want to go—until Miss Sibley, or in this case, the ROTC officers at Grambling, took me by the hand. They tried to explain to me that getting a commission while a reduction was enforced on the military, I might not have much job security, since the first people to go are those who are not regular officers. Normally it takes four years to get your regular-officer status. I'd be up for a regular board after I'd been in four years. So I went for it, and had I not accepted that regular commission, I would have been gone. A lot of kids in my situation had to leave. My career would have been over pretty much before it got started with the big reduction in the mid 1980s.

The grades were always there. But I didn't feel like I was smart. I didn't feel like that woman in uniform I'd seen. Maybe it was the stigma of having been to a black school. I ask myself, would I have competed as well had I gone to a white school?

It seems like my whole life was defined like that. It was always trying to prove that there was more.

It was not until later that I realized it was all God. None of it was about me anyway. I was fighting against something that had absolutely nothing to do with me. It was about Him. When you embrace this idea, it changes your whole life.

But once I joined ROTC, everything just fell into place. I felt like this: the United States Air Force is where I need to be. It was a deeply astonishing revelation.

The thing that did it for me was that *they had confidence in me*, which is something that I was struggling with. I wanted that. I wanted to have the confidence I saw in that officer when she walked across campus. I remember telling my boyfriend, "To me that lady represented an ideal—someone who could smile and encourage you, but if you needed to be disciplined, she could also do that. But, either way, she would never stop treating you like a person." That's how I wanted to be. I wanted to be someone who could command my own sense of presence, hold my own in a conversation, and if it was something that went against my core values, to say, "I'm not having it." I imagined telling that to all the grown-ups who had so disturbed me when I was younger. That woman represented all of that to me.

So I joined the military. At the time, it wasn't about patriotism; it was about my own development as a person and doing something productive with my life. That's what it was about for me. Of course, later I did embrace the idea of patriotic service, of excellence, of all of those principles that I had been taught by my mom. They were not principles the Air Force had to teach me; they were things I embraced because they were the things I believed in. The Air Force gave me the opportunity to become who I really was.

And it started with a bang. One day, I was an undergraduate at Grambling, wondering about what would happen next. But by the time the sun set the next day, I knew what would happen: Overnight, I became a college graduate and a commissioned military officer.

Of course, all I had with me in real terms was a promise of income and a learner's permit. I was on my way, yes, but I didn't have any transportation to get me there. After the graduation ceremony, I was talking to a friend. I explained that I was going to have to report someplace, but I couldn't even drive down the street. I got him to take me to a Chevrolet car lot, because I'd heard of GMAC and somehow I got this idea that if you were in the military doors were going to just open for you. So I went to this car lot without a dime in my pocket, but with every bit of confidence I could summon. That was probably the height of my "I got it going on" attitude. I walked in and of course initially I was told no, I couldn't just take a car and go. After all, I had a commission but I wasn't making any money. I didn't know when my first check was going to come. I told them what I had done and that I was Summa Cum Laude, and that I knew I was going to make it in the military. The salesman said, "That is not going to pay for a car." So what did I do? I asked to speak to the manager. I had a briefcase. I had my transcript. I had all those things. And I had an extra-large attitude. When I left there, I had a car.

The manager said he was going to take a chance on me. I'm not sure what it was, but something I said impressed him. I had a friend drive the car off the lot for me because I didn't want them to know that I wasn't sure I could drive.

I had a permit, but I had never driven by myself.

My whole life had changed because of that black woman in uniform. I carried that inspiration with me when I became a second lieutenant. It was another starting place.

CHAPTER FOUR

AIMING HIGH

I was going to LA, but not the one with the bright lights and great beaches. I was *staying* in LA, as in "Louisiana." The United States Air Force was sending me straight from Grambling, Louisiana, to Alexandria, Louisiana—about two hours and all of 100 miles away. But I was in.

It was my first assignment. I had a supervisor—a black first lieutenant—who was supposed to tell me everything I needed to know about being a great Air Force officer. What he told me was that as an officer I had to look the part. He thought I had to act the part. He took me to, in my opinion, the most expensive places to buy my furniture. He told me what neighborhoods I needed to be in, so we could look only at certain neighborhoods. It tainted some of my expectations because I was coming from a small place with a very small bank account.

I was thinking that if they expected me to look a certain way and act a certain way, then I might not be able to help the people that I wanted to help most. That was a little discouraging at first, because as a second lieutenant I was not making a whole lot of money. Then they asked me to contribute $100 a month to the GI Bill, and they wanted me to be a member of the club, and I had to pay for that. I went in and I still was very modest in doing my apartment. I got a small apartment on the third floor. I was thinking, "People don't have to come to my apartment." I wanted to be able to pay my rent and pay my electricity and have some money left over that I could send home.

Nevertheless, I had, for lack of a better word, *arrived*. I had running water. I turned on the tap and the water was running. Overnight I was out of poverty. The Air Force seemed good to me. (In fact, I think the first time I felt like maybe I had made a wrong decision was when we had the space shuttle crash. I remember sitting on the couch thinking, "It's not over yet. *It's not over.* They're going to find somebody." Prior to this time, nothing like that had happened in our history.) I kept thinking, "I am going into the Air Force—but really, I'm not. I'm just there to get my degree." Somewhere in my young mind, I was still going from high school to college, uncertain, ambivalent, not wanting to commit.

By the time I made first lieutenant and was given my own

account at the US Treasury, I was thinking I should take a picture of the first check that I wrote and send it to my mom, so she could see my signature block on it. I took a picture of it and took it home. I remember telling Mom how I thought a thousand dollars was a lot of money until I had to go to the bank every morning to pick up the cash for the day and they gave me just a handful of hundred dollar bills. I put it in a briefcase. I told her that a thousand dollars doesn't even fill up a briefcase. "It's just one bundle!" When we went to get the cash every morning I'd walk with a briefcase and an armed security guard. It gives the presence that you're really going to take care of some serious business. It made me feel important, but I wasn't. Second lieutenant or first lieutenant—I wasn't making a whole lot of money.

Courtroom Drama

One of the first things I had to do in the Air Force was sit on a court martial. I remember the case because it helped me learn to make decisions. It was about an enlisted couple. They were in two different squadrons, and they had had a spat. She had accused him of brandishing a weapon, and she told her first sergeant. They were trying to discharge her husband. Her husband was the father of her child and they brought the child in. They even had the child testify. He had to have been no more than five or six years old.

According to the little boy, he did do it, but it was obviously not really as serious as they made it out to be in the trial. Nobody felt threatened, and it got blown completely out of proportion. We found him guilty of brandishing the weapon and he got court martialed—but I saw the lasting effect on their family. I think we did more damage than anything because by the end, the wife was there trying to defend her husband and the child.

I wish I could have followed them, found out what happened after that, but it left a really bad taste in my mouth. Remember, I came from a family where my mom loved my dad and my dad loved my mom, even though they got in arguments, and once, I saw him take a swing at her. Some people stay, and some people don't. I guess my people stay—no matter what.

A Married Officer

I had a lot of people tell me, even as I announced my engagement, that I shouldn't marry my husband. But one thing I had not learned very well was how to let things go. So I dug in, because my family taught me that when you make your bed, you sleep in it. My friends thought he was too old. Art was not an officer. He was civilian—but he had been in the military, which I thought was a good thing. And he had been married once.

We met at England Air Force Base. Art managed a warehouse. His office was right behind the finance office. We would often play volleyball out in that little area so he saw me there playing volleyball with his crew, and he asked people if anyone knew who that new lieutenant was.

I didn't know him, and he didn't know me, but we were coming up on an inspection from the inspector general, or IG, so some of our people asked permission to hide all the stuff we needed to get rid of in his warehouse. That way we'd put on a good show for the IG. The inspection came and went, but many months later our stuff was *still* in that warehouse. I didn't know anything about it, but I knew Art's lieutenant and Art's lieutenant knew me. One day he said to Art, "Hey. Go across the street and talk to Lieutenant Evans (my maiden name) and find out when they're going to get that stuff out of our warehouse."

I was at work, when somebody said, "Hey! There's a guy here wants to see Lt. Evans."

I said, "Wants to see me? What for? And who is it, anyway?"

I come out of the office and I start looking up and I can't stop looking up because there's this six-foot, two-inch guy—I'm five foot three—standing there looking down at me and he's saying, "You've got to get your stuff out of my warehouse." I didn't even know what he was talking about.

I said, "Is it ours?"

"It's yours." His manner and the way he spoke seemed to say, *I'm here for a mission. This is what I want done.*

I didn't know what to do. So I said, "One moment please." I knew it wasn't me that he really wanted so I started to go and get our deputy but he said, "Oh no, no, I made this agreement to see Lt. Evans. That's *you.*"

"I don't know what you're talking about."

I'm cracking up. The whole conversation changed. He was pushy, and I had to push back. Well, after that, of course, he started asking around to find out who I was and pretty soon he was telling me I wanted to go out to dinner. I kept saying no, I didn't. This went on for a while until the civilian pay chief, Ms. Gladys, who worked for me at the time, said, "Myra, I know Art. He's okay. Why don't you give him a shot?"

I said, "I'm really not interested." I was trying to be nice but he called one day on the phone and said, "Just tell me what form a person has to fill out to get a meeting with you?" You see I was strictly about business.

I did finally accept a dinner date at an all-you-can-eat seafood place in Alexandria. It was almost a disaster because I didn't eat seafood. I just never tried it. I get to the restaurant and I'm thinking, "Now what am I going to do?" Most of the stuff on the menu I had never eaten and he was pushing stuff I'd never heard of. "You've got to try salt licks, you've got to try this, try that"—and I'm thinking, "Oh, man, how am I going to get through this night?" But I was trying to be nice—and believe it or not I found that I love shrimp. I also found that the frog legs were tolerable—like they say, tastes like chicken. There is a first time for everything.

After that, there were many, many nights of talking on the phone about life, and about his daughters. He told me about his divorce. He talked a lot that first night about his passion for his girls and how the divorce had separated them. I thought it was very interesting that a man would share that kind of information, so I thought maybe he's not so bad after all.

Six months later Art asked me to marry him. Of course, coming from a small town, and being a country girl, I said, "Hey, not without asking my dad. We have got to go through the whole nine yards."

We invited Mom and Dad down. Art told them his intentions. That next February, February 14, 1987, we got married. I had always wanted to get married on Valentine's Day and have at least a six-month relationship with the person before I married. It all went as I had hoped.

The whole thing was very surreal, but we did it. My mom came up to me later and said, "The best advice I can give you is that, baby, if you love the man, you have to accept that he has kids. That's a part of who he is."

And she was right, again.

The Money Secret

Personal financial responsibility was huge in my family and in my whole make-up. When I learned that my husband had been bankrupt I did not tell anybody. It took me a long time to forgive him and to understand that life happens. We all go through things that if we had an opportunity to do it over, we'd do it differently. But in the back of my mind, I held that against him, and so of course, I took over all our finances.

Once Art got a job he was back on track. It's just that when we would first move, he wouldn't have a job, so we would go from two incomes to one every time we moved. And as a military family, that was often. The challenge was keeping it all together, all those periods of time when he wasn't working.

It was very difficult because I had higher expectations, not only for my troops and for the people under my command, but I especially had high expectations for my marriage, my husband, and everything else in my personal life. It was very, very challenging for me to try to balance having a family and having a career in this man-dominant world. I would think, *hey, I deserve your respect because I earned it and I spent time earning it. Not because I was a woman. Not because I was black. You followed me not just because I wore the oak leaf clusters; you followed me because I earned your respect and I was taking you down a path that was the right path to follow.* Yes, everyone got the same Myra, and my husband probably got it worst.

Far From Louisiana

We got an overseas assignment. I was excited to be finally going away from Louisiana. I thought this little girl is going to *finally* get out of Louisiana. It was just my husband and me. We went to Germany in 1989 the first time. We stayed until 1992.

When Art had suggested we go overseas, I didn't want to go. But when he said, "Hey I think our careers would do well if we just follow a plan." I listened.

Things didn't work out for Art as he had hoped, because, as it had been in America, it was difficult for him to get a job. They wanted to know *everything*, every time we moved. He'd have to go through the same song and dance. Most of his enlisted friends were the same. They all wanted to know what it was like being married to an officer. He'd say, "When she walks in the door, the uniform goes off and all I have is my wife." That was a good answer, and I thought he had a good perspective on it. There were often times behind closed doors he would have to say to me, "Listen: I'm not your airman. I'm not one of your troops."

When we first arrived, though, we were so excited. I had one of the best sponsors. She had already found me a house "on the economy"—which is to say, in Air Force parlance, in a German house with a German landlord—so I could move right in. She made sure I knew about the culture and where to go shop. She had stuff already in my apartment. She had already had the rental furniture delivered! We were able to move right into our house. Art started looking for work. It looked like it was going to be a smooth transition.

Two weeks later, almost two weeks to the day, I got a call in the middle of the night. Our acting first sergeant was on the line. "The Red Cross is trying to reach you." My dad had had a stroke. The next day I talked to my sisters and they said, "Myra, we need you to come home. You've got to come home. It's that bad."

I finally made it back to America and to the hospital. My family was all there, but I still didn't understand the gravity of the whole situation. I went in, talked to my Dad, of course—and that's when I found out that he was in a coma. He had had a major stroke. When they first contacted me, the only activity was in his brain stem, but that didn't mean anything to me at the time. I have since learned that he was only holding on by a thread and they kept him alive until I made it there. They did not take him off life support until I had returned home.

It was very difficult for me. Of course, I wanted to stay with Mom. We had started building a home for them, so they could get out of that three-room shack. They were still living in that. My dad had added a room, though, for us kids, because we had gotten too big to be in the same room with our parents. So, when my oldest sister and I had started to work, the first thing we did was pool our resources and took Mom down to have a custom home built, one with three bedrooms. It was small. It was modest. It was actually done in Mom and Dad's name. The interest rate, of course, was higher, but it was something that they would own. It was a dream come true.

When Dad died, we were afraid Mom would never move into the house because it had not been finished. We still had to have the water put in and the pipes laid and all of that. Thank God for my brothers-in-law and my husband. We all came together and got it done.

My husband still wasn't working. I took out an advance of $3,000, and do you know, looking back, it was all God's plan: by taking that advance out, I had the resources to help Mom bury Dad and get settled in the new home. Of course, that wasn't what the advance was for, but when you start where you are and use what you have... God does the rest.

It was, however, probably one of the biggest blows in my career. At that point I thought, "This all sounded good and great, but I'm too far away now. Who's going to help Mom? Yes, Dad had his problems; he'd drink way too much, smoke too much, all of those things, but Dad was *there*." At the time we often asked Mom, "Why are you putting up with this drinking and all of this stuff?" But you know, when we look back on it, my sisters and I realize some people don't even have a dad. They don't know him— wouldn't even recognize him. I think being there meant a lot. Dad's influence kept us on the straight and narrow.

It cost a lot, in that my father never had a steady job. He

never earned enough to get social security. When dad died, everybody around thought, "Oh, they're going to come into money now." We were having a house built, so everybody assumed that we were building that on Dad's social security. They had no idea. We didn't get anything. My baby sister was ten years old; she couldn't draw it. Nobody could draw anything because there was nothing to draw.

Nothing had really changed. My sister was ten, and my Mom was left to raise her alone. My sister got into a lot of things; I didn't realize the impact of not having a dad around. We grew up with Dad in the house. My little sister went everywhere with him. If he had to go for an errand for my grandmother, anything, he took the baby with him. Everybody knew her in Coushatta, and she knew everybody. All of a sudden her dad is taken and there was nobody there for her. She became a different person.

She went through a lot of things. She finally told us that there were people who had abused her. Well, my mom didn't want to believe it and she thought my sister was just acting out. I remember I was overseas when my mom called me and told me, and I had to say, "Mom, it's true." I knew it was true, because I knew I had been there. I never told her any details, I just said, "Mamma, it's true." She said if my dad were still alive, he'd kill them. She's probably right, and that's probably why we never said anything. I would never want to hurt my mom like that, and back then people would just say, "Oh, you know, that's just old drunk so and so, you know he don't mean anything." Yeah, so-and-so was a drunk, but does that make it right? We know now it happens and probably more often than the black community ever admitted.

CHAPTER FIVE

BACK ON DUTY

My father's death was a wake-up call. I felt an even greater urgency to succeed than before. I had to do something. I had to go make something happen. I no longer had a dad. It was up to me now. I think I took it on.

You throw your whole self into your work when a tragedy like that happens. In an odd way, you make a new start. Mom had told me, "Myra, your dad was really proud of you, and he would want you to go back." I knew I had to go back to work. That's all I knew. And really that's all I wanted to know. I was going to be the best that I could be. I worked long hours. When the Gulf War kicked off, it was just work, work, work, *work*. And my husband didn't get a job right away either. I didn't realize the impact that was having on him. I said, "You should be happy. I'm working. It's going to happen."

And then sure enough it did happen. He got a job, but by then I had withdrawn so much from the relationship that I was happy for him getting a job, but it was like, I got to do this whether you get a job or not. He needed me to be there but even when I was, I wasn't.

Committed at Last

Once I made the decision that I was going to stay in the Air Force, I knew I had to really, really give it my all. I would look at others, my peers, and they seemed to have always gotten recognition. So I left Germany the first time and I went back to the states, to K.I. Sawyer, an SAC base in Michigan. I was struggling. I needed to find myself and start from there. So I asked myself, "Why are you feeling this? Is it because you're a woman? Is it because you're black?" I had a hard time following orders blindly; I needed to understand more of why we were doing what we did.

Of course, that didn't always go very well. I left there and went to the headquarters at Air Combat Command in Langley, Virginia. Again, I was not in my core career. I was in what is called operations and "operations" in the Air Force means pilots. All the funding that I had, all the projects that I worked on, were in direct support of the pilots. Again, I found myself in a culture that made no sense to me. I was an *accountant*. How could I, in the career field that I was in, rise above all of that and make myself known as somebody who needs to be recognized?

We went back to Germany to Spangdahlem, and they finally promoted me, but that meant a pilot had been passed over. He complained. That was so devastating to me. I remember talking to my supervisor, Elaine Kingston, a white supervisor and one of the best people I know—she became my son's godmother. She was a super great person. I have lots of respect for her, even to this day. I asked her to be my son's godmother because I was under her when I went through a lot of fertility treatments. When I couldn't have a child and prior to making the decision to adopt Elaine gave me the time to actually go to the hospital to do the fertility treatments. Another thing she did, too, that I don't think anybody else would have done: The Air Force in those days did not give leave to a person who adopted a child. If you gave birth, you got four to six weeks off. But in 1996, you didn't get that if you adopted a child.

But she went to the two-star general commanding the directorate and said, "She needs time to be with this baby." He approved it. She gave me projects to work on at home so I could be off with my son. God put the right person in my path at the right time. She accepted being a godmother for my son. She came to our all-black church and stood there with us. I had a black godmother on one side, the lady who had introduced me to my husband, and I had Elaine on the other side with her husband. For some it might seem like what they did in high school, when they had the "black-every-award," but for me it was not about race; I believe for the Kingstons it was about reaching across to help someone because it's decent and it's the right thing to do. And that was the start of something beautiful, right where we were.

Desert Storm

When Desert Storm broke out, it meant that at Spangdahlem we worked long hours. We were responsible for ensuring that people were processed through the line and got paid. All that had to be set up. A lot of people came back, of course, with pay problems, and that affected the families left behind—we had changed the laws from earlier wars where a family member could not come in during a member's deployment and change a person's pay.

It was complicated: When an airman was deployed, the pay was set up, and that was how it had to be. On the line, however, you were told to have your legal documents —powers of attorney and things like that—so if you were killed or incapacitated, your rights could be protected. So we had legal people talking to us and making requests.

Everybody on this line is preparing to process out, and members from our unit were saying, "Hey, we're not going to be able to talk to your wife or your spouse, so make sure you have an account set up where they have access."

I remember talking with the squadron and telling them, "Don't take your job lightly. Don't think all you do is payroll, because what you are doing is just as important as those out on the flight line. When people leave family behind, they need to know that their pay is taken care of, that we're going to pay them on time every month because sometimes that's the only way their family is going to eat if their breadwinner is no longer there."

We went into educational mode. It was very important to me that people going out knew what they could and could not do, and what we were going to be able to help them with. The F16s deployed out of Spangdahlem and went down range, so it was lots and lots of long hours, lots of processing. While I didn't deploy, the whole base was constantly in that mode. That was our goal. Our goal was to make sure everything went as planned.

I bled blue at that time. I was so involved in the Air Force as a career, as a way of living, that I thought everybody around me should feel the same way. Everything else went on hold. That's a mistake I think a lot of us made, and continue to make, and I think that's something that women in particular feel even more so than their male counterparts—especially if we have a family. Women want to be the best that we can be, and sometimes the job just doesn't stop. I would see my male counterparts at early morning stand up and late night stand up, and I felt like they did not have the same stressors. I saw that they were going to go home and their wife had the food cooked, they had their house cleaned, everything was done. They didn't have to deal with those things. Don't get me wrong; my husband helped me a lot in those areas, but mostly because I just wasn't there to do it. I don't think it was so much to help lighten my load. I was still the "woman," the wife, the mother, etc. And if he didn't say that exactly, I still thought it was all mine to handle.

By the time I went back to the US, I was so ready to leave Germany. I was exhausted. I felt that I had done all I could do for the squadron. I loved the squadron. We had achieved awards. I just felt like I had no more to give. I wanted to return to the states. I was excited about it, and I needed it. In order to grow in the Air Force you need breath. I needed to experience something different.

Nobody knew me in the states, so my boss made a phone call when we found K.I. Sawyer was open. They had a military budget office, and they had a civilian chief. He knew the squadron commander and made a phone call, asking if he'd be willing to take me on. He agreed because he respected my commander. I was excited about that. I was excited to be able to continue my career and do another phase of comptrollership. We left in July, just before Independence Day.

Hurricane Andrew

A few months later, of course, Hurricane Andrew, one of the most destructive storms to ever hit the US, struck. I was deployed (my only official deployment) to Tent City, a thrown-together temporary camp built in the rubble left behind by the hurricane. After that experience, I could say to people, "Only God knows what you can take." He taught me my lessons along the way without having to deploy overseas to a war zone. I salute those who did, and I thank them for their sacrifice and service.

Being in Tent City was a huge eye opener for me because I had never seen anything like that. I came from Louisiana, and we had storms. But this was different. I felt like I had been sheltered all my life in a little capsule, but having to go through something like the aftermath of Andrew, and to see all of the mud and the devastation from a hurricane, it actually looked like a war zone. I could not imagine a war zone that didn't look like what I was facing, because everything I could see was trashed. Even the airplanes that were mounted on pedestals around the base were all on the ground. When I went to the office where the comptroller used to be, I was knee deep in mud. All of the papers were ruined, and the only things that were saved were in the vault. But the place was horrible; I couldn't have explained it any other way.

It was the worst feeling. I sent pictures home, and I told my mom and my sister, you had to be there to believe it. Even the TV coverage did not do it justice when the news crews went around. Walking into it, I wondered, "How did anyone survive?" Seeing that much devastation on a military base in the United States was hard to deal with. I think one of the reasons I was there was because I had not lived through it and I hadn't personally lost anything, so I was able to come in and take care of the money issues without being emotionally involved.

At that time, we had a phenomenal team that came in to steer a steady course. This made me realize the importance of what the military does, and why it needs people it can count on. We were there to help our brothers and sisters. That's the way we took it. In the early days when we went, there weren't a lot of tents to go around, so I actually slept in the tent with the money. My escort stayed there too. He stayed on one side and I stayed on the other side. Initially I don't think they knew the three of us stayed together. We had a guard, a cashier, and me. They let me have one half of the tent by myself and then they shared the other half. They were enlisted. It was very unusual. But I did not have any reservations. I knew what the mission was, and I think they did too.

Hurricane Andrews goes down as one of the worst disasters in the history of the United States. It destroyed the entire base and to this day we still don't have Homestead, which had been a huge base. Andrew destroyed it all—all the housing, everything.

I went back to K.I. Sawyer. The major was so glad to be getting me back that he had them put up banners!

But my commander was more difficult than I first thought. He didn't seem to have the ability to issue clear commands. So when he said, "Do something," we would have to figure out what he meant and how to make it happen. And every day that got harder and harder to do. The level of insensitivity was amazing. Sometimes, he would say something and then do something to which the only reaction was *ouch!* How could I continue to support a person when my toes were being stepped on over and over again?

There was the issue of raising money for the booster club.

My boss was a civilian, and he did not like doing that. He was a resident of K.I. Sawyer. I've never seen anybody get so upset. My commander cursed and said, "I'm sick and tired of these civilians who don't want to do anything." He said, "I'm going to fix them when it comes rating time."

I thought, "Wow, it's really not that big of a deal," so I said, "Hey, boss, I understand what you're saying. Yeah, sometimes they don't want to do what we in the military want done, but really you may want to tone it down about the appraisal, because we can't really document anything like that in the appraisal."

He just went on about how sick and tired he was of it. Okay, he was blowing off steam—but then later I would see things that made me question his character. For example, if we were in a staff meeting and a female passed by, he would literally just lean over in his chair, leaning out the door watching her and I'm thinking, "Really boss, don't be so obvious, you've got people around. People are talking."

I tried to help. At first I would go into his office and talk to him and say, "Hey, maybe there was a better way we could have addressed this or that." But it was hard to keep up with him! For example, there was a female lieutenant in our organization that he thought the world of; he thought she was everything. A technical sergeant was in charge of having the squadron plaque redone. The favorite lieutenant was going to be the first one to get the new plaque, and the commander didn't like it. When they presented it to him, to show him what they had come up with and what they were going to give her, he threw it in the trash can in front of the enlisted guy and started cursing. He just went off and said he wouldn't give that to his worst enemy and it was this, that and the other. But somebody in the squadron had designed it, had come up with it, had totally done the woodworking stuff. The enlisted guy and I thought that was the worst thing a commander could do.

It was so cruel. It was a small thing, but he kept compounding mistakes like that. For example, he wanted us to use appropriated dollars to buy the emblem for the plaque. But that's against regulations. I tried to explain that there was no wiggle room for us to do this, and my supervisor had discussed it with him as well. He pretty much felt that, because he was commander, he could order us to break the regulations. We refused, and all of these things started adding up for me until I said to myself, "Okay, one last-ditch effort. I'll take the lieutenant with me, and we'll go meet him, and talk about these things."

He wanted us to meet him at the club, so we went. I told him all about these things and that I was really concerned that maybe we were overstepping our authority. He went on to plead his case, and he actually started crying. I was really getting a little concerned, because he was taking everything I said so personally. This is not good.

I said, "Well, if we can't come to an agreement on this, I think I'm going to take it up the chain, and bring it up to somebody else." He said that he doesn't remember me saying that, but I know that I told him, and that was my last option. I felt I needed to go up because I needed to stand up for the people in the squadron.

The next morning after I slept on it, my spirit said, "Go forward, because he's not going to change. He doesn't think he did anything wrong and he's still defending it." Well, the worst mistake I've ever made in my career was to go to his supervisor. He was a colonel. I sat and I talked to him and explained the situation. He looked at me and said, "Well, Myra, when there's a gray area, we always side with the commander." He told me I had to figure out how to get along with him. He hadn't done anything illegal, immoral, or unethical.

I agreed reluctantly. I had to pull myself together, because I was emotional at this time. It was like having cold water thrown in my face. I thought, "How stupid of me to come up here, knowing this." I went back to the office and pulled myself together, and the next morning I knew that the boss had called him and told him I had been in his office.

In fact, I found out later through the IG report that the colonel called them before I even showed up, told them I was on his calendar, and asked what it was about. From that point it went downhill, because when I went back to the office, the commander kicked me out of the staff meeting. He told me he didn't want to see me any more in his staff meetings; he didn't want anything to do with me. Every opportunity he got to show me that I was beneath him, he took.

Once, he had to go on leave, and when a commander goes on leave, he has to leave his organization in the control of someone else, because if something happens in the squadron to an enlisted person, someone has to have command authority to take action. I was the next ranking person in the squadron. He refused to pass the baton to me. When he left, the paperwork had to go to the legal office to make sure that the baton was being passed appropriately, and they had to sign off on it.

They wouldn't sign off on it. Instead, they called and asked, "Is Myra there?" Our guy told them, "Yes, she's here, but the commander wants to pass the baton to somebody else." They said, "Well, he can't do that." Our guy said, "Well, she's working on a special project." He used that as an excuse for not giving me the command. The legal office said that wasn't good enough, and that I had to be put on those orders. I knew that the boss didn't want me on them, but I accepted them because that's what the legal office said. When the commander got back, he tore into the guy who had made the change according to what legal said and told him, "Next time I leave here, and I leave something to be done, that's exactly what I expect. I don't want her in charge." The guy knew that he didn't want me to have it, but he was on this commander's support staff, so the guy was very tight lipped and did not want to say exactly what the major had said, because he feared what would happen.

I would lock myself away when he would get vocal. In front of people, I had to muster up enough gumption to act as if his behavior was okay and try to figure out a way to support him. I would give this front, but then I would have to go to the bathroom, and just cry my eyes out and then dry my tears, try to get myself back together before I would face troops again. At lunch time, instead of eating I would go over to a sister's house, a member of our church, and she would pray with me during lunch, so I could go back to work and face it again. It was a nightmare. I'd go home in the evening and I'd walk through the doors in my house, and my husband would just stand there and let me fall into his arms, because it was so stressful. He and my mom wanted to fix it. My mom was telling me to be careful: "Be careful, Myra. Watch your tires. Your tires could be cut." She just didn't trust the guy. If he did all of that, she was afraid that he would do something else. At this point, I'll be honest with you: I didn't think he would be above any of that, so I started trying to leave.

I finally got out. In 1994, I left K.I. Sawyer for Langley Air Force Base, which was fortunate because it brought Elaine Kingston back into my life. She was a budget officer when I first met her at England Air Force Base. She had been promoted, and she had her own little office at Langley Air Force Base. She knew my work ethic, and she said that she wanted me. She called and asked me if I wanted a job. I said, "If you could work that, that would be *great*. I would love to come and work for you."

She set out and tried to get me there to help her stand up that organization. When she called the assignment people and was so adamant requesting me by name, they told her they didn't know why she wanted me because the commander said I was a troublemaker. Well, that sent up red flags. She called me in, and I decided to share with her everything that was going on. I told her everything. Once she heard what I had to say, she was even more determined to get me, so she went in and talked to her two-star general. When a two-star speaks we listen. He called the assignment people and said that I was who he wanted, so they cut orders and sent me there. What I didn't know at the time was that I had been pretty much blacklisted in my career field. They wouldn't hire me at the headquarters in my career field. But getting hired into the Operations Directorate turned out to be a pivotal point in my career.

Once I got there, I started decompressing from all the stress I had been under. The two-star general reviewed my record because my supervisor told me I needed to go and talk to him concerning my chances of getting promoted to major. Because of the way the previous commander had written my last report, and because I did not get a medal when I left there, my chances of getting promoted were pretty much slim to none. I had to make a decision. So what were my options? They told me I could get the report thrown out—but if I got it thrown out, my record was going to be missing a report and the promotion board would wonder what happened. It would leave too much speculation.

My other option was to try to get them to give me the award and then pray that the reports I earned at Langley would be strong enough to overcome that particular one. The two-star general said he believed I had a case for the IG, and he supported me on writing my IG report. He just cautioned me to stay very factual. I filed the IG complaint, saying that he had denied me a medal because of personality conflict, not because of my performance.

The IG did find that there were some issues with how things were handled. I requested a copy of that report through the Freedom of Information Act. The report had been very heavily redacted. There were no names in it, no who-said-what, but based on the questions that the IG asked and based on the responses of the people, I kind of know who said what in the big scheme of things. For example, I know when the vice commander spoke, because he talked about how I came to him and what he saw next. He talked about how I used to be very outgoing and then I seemed to be reserved, and so the IG asked him, "Did you think anything strange of that since she had come to you? Did you find it strange that she wasn't the same person she was and all of that?" His response was that he felt I could or should have come back to him. It was really sickening to read the report. In the end, I could not get the recommendations of the IG. They redacted all of that, so none of the recommendations are in there. However, I did find out that the guy retired as a major. I ended up getting a medal, and this guy retired as a major, so what does that say? To me it says there was enough in the report to say that he had overstepped his bounds.

> In the Air Force, I also learned that nobody will do anything for you if you aren't willing to care about them first. In other words, I use the saying, "People don't care how much you know until they know how much you care." My success in the military was not about what I had done; it was about what I was doing. That was important to me because at that time I was struggling with my self-esteem. I learned to take the chip off my shoulder, stand tall, be confident, and go out and lead.

I saw him later, after I had made lieutenant colonel. I went up to him in a meeting and I said, "Hi, sir?" I still said "sir." I spoke to him and everything. This was after he retired. He just smiled and spoke with me briefly. He was at a table with other people, and I have to say that it felt good to me. There will be some bumps along the way when you get started, but start you must and do what you can, and sometimes good really does trump evil.

Becoming a Mom

Speaking of promotions, Langley is where I started and finished the adoption process that led me to motherhood. I had discovered I wasn't able to have a child. Part of it could have been all the stress; I don't know. The doctors couldn't find anything wrong, but I wasn't able to conceive. I finally decided that I wanted to talk to my husband, and we started talking about adoption. We submitted the paperwork in October 1995. In April 1996, I was bringing home my son.

I discovered that adopting a child in a black community is not that easy. Blacks don't generally put their children up for adoption; they usually give children to somebody else in the family. We don't give up our children easily so there's often not enough black parents for the black children who do get put up for adoption. I went to a Catholic charity. It was definitely outside my religious upbringing, but I liked them because they provided alternatives to abortion.

That whole process of writing letters to a prospective mother and talking about why I would want a child, and how we would raise a child, and all the required statements was an experience I really enjoyed. We had home studies, counseling, and all these things. We were hoping and praying.

I was in a meeting when I got the phone call. Somebody said, "Your husband is trying to reach you. It's important." I went outside to take the call. A moment later, I had to go back to the meeting and say, "I'm sorry, I have an emergency. I have to leave," and I left. It was a working group meeting, and I don't like to miss working groups, but I left. The agency asked if we could come down—they thought they had a baby for me. I went down there and I'm telling you, I instantly fell in love with this little boy. It was one of the happiest days of my life. The day I saw him, I knew

I wanted *that* baby. I wanted to bring him home, and the next day when we went to pick him up, I showed up with a diaper bag with everything in it—because on our way out I had gone and bought everything. I was going to be a mother. And this changed everything!

End of My Air Force Career

I met a lot of people in those years, and many of them were remarkable. Colonel Mary K. Hertog was one. She was a tall, tall lady and a no-nonsense person. I truly admired her. She reminded me of Col. Armour-Lightner from my ROTC days. She had that great sense of presence. She was always engaged and was very well respected. Working for her was a true joy, because she didn't waste time. She knew we had a life, and she wanted us to get to our families, too. We worked long hours, but it was productive time.

There were five things that made her an excellent officer. One was her mantra—"Mission first, people always." It didn't matter the mission, you always felt important as a person. Another thing: She believed that it's okay to be human and be an officer. We smiled a lot and talked about our kids—she about her cat. Three, I learned that in the midst of a trying time I can be confident, disciplined, and still take care of people. When we lost one of our own, she was human and a leader. Four: The importance of the smallest detail—she had an eye for seeing what others missed, because she was engaged and she paid attention. Fifth: I worked for her because she knew I had her back, and she had mine.

When I met Colonel Hertog in 2004, I was almost bitter with the Air Force because a colonel had been allowed to stay on when he was so abusive to so many people—including me. I didn't think we were holding our senior officers accountable. When Mary K. Hertog came along, she put respect back into command. She found worth in the worst; she discovered what they could do and let them do it. And when they didn't, she held them accountable. It turned everything around. The morale went from someplace in the toilet to the highest it had ever been. I attribute that to her leadership. She didn't make it about her or me or anyone; it was everyone as an integral part of the team—Mission first, people always! In 2004, she was promoted to brigadier general.

When it was time for me to retire, I had plenty of commanders to choose from, but General Hertog was the one I wanted to officiate at my retirement. I told her why: that she gave me back respect for command. I could have spent twenty years and walked out the door, and been very, very bitter about the Air Force. That's where I was, but in my last year, she gave me more than I ever could have asked for. I didn't want to spend my life doing something, only to be bitter when I left. She made me feel that, as a person, I had contributed, that I was worth something. My career had not been in vain. For that, I will be forever grateful. And so as I neared the end of my time in the Air Force, I found it was once again time to start again.

CHAPTER SIX

THE SOLUTION LIES WITHIN

One of the most wonderful things the Air Forces teaches you is the benefits of diversity—how to embrace other people's gifts and talents and put them all on a winning team. I found out how important this was as a commander, and along the way I uncovered a few gifts and talents of my own.

In the Air Force, you are not promoted based on what you can individually accomplish; working late and taking work home doesn't matter as much as the success of the team you lead. The team matters most—whether it's a squadron, or the entire military. Individuals may be heroic and perform remarkable, even history-making, feats. But no one plans for heroism to save the day. The Air Force rightly teaches you that no war is won by a single officer, just as no battle is won by a single individual. A smart officer knows that the right strategy is not to hope for individual heroism but to give the team the leadership it needs to win. That's what works. That became very apparent to me early on, so I understood my role as a leader was to help build a team that can reach a common goal by working together. That has always been very, very important to me.

As time passed, I saw people come and go in and out of the military, and soon I realized that not everyone has that shared vision of what leadership is all about. That can matter a great deal when transitioning out and back to civilian life, because sometimes a military role doesn't translate very well to the outside world. Does that make me less of a person? Absolutely not. I think the military has some of the most disciplined, well-educated people anywhere, people who are able to look at situations and make good decisions, even without having all the facts. *The key is always leadership.*

The Partnership Team

Teams come in all sizes. What matters most is how well they succeed. Leading well is what our business is all about. I met Loeka several years ago. We had been together for about eight years, working together to implement a new performance management and compensation system under the same program executives. Our skill sets are totally different. I'm more of a policy nerd and a by-the-checklist manager, used to pulling things together from different sources, while he is truly an innovative, creative type.

I remember our executive used to call him a genius. I said, "Well, okay, he's a genius—but he can't stay on-task." That was my military background talking, since the Air Force is all about staying on-task. You give us a task and a checklist, and we'll get it done.

I think Loeka was trying to prove to me that everything should be based on models and research. But when he would bring me some, I thought, harebrained idea, I would ask him for a source document: "No source document? We can't just make up stuff. We have got to have a source." I always did my research before I did anything else. But he was a doctoral candidate at Texas A&M University, so for him, models mattered because everything was about theory.

Finally, I asked him one day, "What are you going to do with all this education when you grow up?" I kept saying we needed to put his theories into practice and see if they really worked. I repeated my question: "Tell me, what exactly, do you really want to do?" What he later explained to me is that life is a living theory; we operate in a system that's made of many model(s) whether it's your mental model or the service model we manage.

He started talking about this idea for a platform that would help the community. That actually made sense! That's when we started working together.

We started by looking at launching a small business because, at the time, everybody was saying to veterans that they had to transition to civilian life—because at the time, politicians claimed we needed a smaller military. This claim always comes and goes. The defense budget is always a big political target because it's such a huge slice of the budget.

As a veteran, I experienced the change myself—veterans transitioning back to civilian life creates lots of variables. The best-laid plans can go into the trashcan overnight, because suddenly there's a new need, a new goal. So what were we to do? We needed to figure that out, because not knowing how to lead is leading many people straight to failure. Yet there are so many resources out there—and a lot of money—all aimed at helping people succeed. It was a paradox.

Our research team got together and we started looking at the problems faced by these businesses. We started talking to people, and we started going to different places, always asking the question, "What is causing common problems?"

Our research showed us that while the resources to help existed, what was missing was *collaboration*. What we were missing was the ability to recognize that people can't do it alone, whether a soldier, airman or small business person. So how are you aligning yourself with others who don't have what you have, or with people who need what you have? If you are not building collaboration and cooperation, what are you doing?

Our primary goal is to create a platform where small businesses can come and engage with others to discover the root causes for their main failure points and find solutions to help them succeed. If I'm a small business and I don't do accounting or whatever, that's one of my failure points. I don't have the right people on the team.

Or, a small business may be great with HR and hiring practices but need help and advice in other areas. I can come in and put together useful suggestions for you. All of this is at a cost, but it's not at a cost to break the bank. I don't have to have seven individuals on my staff if I've aligned myself on this platform. That's what we're looking at doing, testing some technology solutions that would benefit everybody. Instead of everybody learning the same lessons by failing and getting out of business, we were looking at ways to use the challenges to learn and benefit all.

Global e-Talent Network 7.0

I'm one of the co-founders of Global e-Talent Network 7.0, LLC or GeTN7 for short. The number 7 is intentional in that it refers to the number of perfection or completeness in the bible. We want to help "complete" or perfect the goals of our clients. GeTN7 is based on a proprietary concept that we created. It's a business model we use to bring people in at any point and help them figure out what pain-points their business have, and then find out what can be done to relieve that pain. If it's financial, then we can help them with that. That's one aspect of it.

The second aspect of the business and perhaps the core is providing the research and development needed for businesses to get started and stay viable. For example, we help business leaders and individuals develop the skill set and technology solutions required, based on specific set of requirements. It's ideal for those who do not have access to the resources, time, or expertise necessary to create an innovative solution, something that will help them proceed strategically with a business plan or idea that they can translate into dollars. It's this process of monetization that elevates a great idea and produces a great business. We think that's the key to a business survival, an individual transitioning from one career to another, or the launch of a brand new idea. During secondary research, we discovered a report published by the National Association for Women Business Owners (NAWBO) that revealed pain points we could help others frame into a problem statement worth solving with creative and innovative solutions. Then we set out to design an accelerated camp (ACE Camp for short) to elevate ideas into marketable solutions.

Case Study 1: The Nehemiah Project

A local church had committed to a very impressive project to talk about recidivism issues a few years ago. They had involved many organizations, launched it, run it for a year and then asked us for input. They said, "We really want to get to what people believe the problems are. What do they need? How do they reenter society? What are they missing?" Those are great questions.

So we partnered with them, asked them to spell out their goals, and we helped them set up focus groups to address "What keeps you up at night?" It was a resounding success, and now we are continuing with them to implement some of the ideas they got from the focus groups, measuring their success with data, and then using the data to iterate and actually solve real issues. That church has become a part of the solution in the community by actually listening to the people who are trying to reenter from incarceration. It's a great example of how to start where you are, use what you have, and do what you can.

Case Study 2: The Family Investment Project

We respond energetically when people come to us with great ideas. For example, we met a veteran who wanted to improve investment education in the black community, because so many of us are so afraid of the market. Many of us don't even think of investing beyond our 401(k) or something like that. He was a self-taught, military veteran who raised his kids to "get off the runway." They are all in business on their own—plus they're working, *plus* they have this healthy relationship with the market. They all have done very well. He wanted to help more people "get off the runway," which is what he called having $100,000 in a portfolio.

The problem: He was a very traditional investor who wanted to reach more young people, but he didn't know how to use technology. He was super successful but did it all with pen and paper and published information. To help him expand, we helped him put together a whole program that worked more quickly and efficiently by introducing him to investment technology and mobile communication that allows him to stay in contact with his customers no matter where they are.

He taught us as much as we taught him. He knew how to simplify investment language, making it much easier for other people to learn what he knows. In return, we helped give him a business model and a platform that he could present, so that people were able to get his information and make the life changes he advocated. In fact, just by making the information available in a way that was marketable and reachable by a whole new generation, he was able to connect with more people including those who could help him get the word out, and second, who could help him design the workbook and other materials he wanted to create.

Today

Our business is almost four years old. We launched in 2012 with just enough capital to file the license and we have earned revenue. However, we also had failures along the way. But what we learned is how to turn those failures into opportunities to iterate and pivot to keep going. Our goal was and is to build something useful. I am so proud that we are walking this journey ourselves. When I tell you that failing fast is not a bad thing, I know what that means, and I know why it's so important, because if you never try and fail, you can never improve. I can now fully embrace the importance of innovation.

The world turns and the market changes daily. Whether you are a small business, a transitioning veteran, a church, or anyone looking to change directions, you need to do research and look at data on a regular basis and compare with others like you. If you do not know there's a problem to solve or you don't know what that problem is—then, yes, you're not going to last. You can succeed only if you are helping reduce somebody's pain or fulfilling a need. Take a twenty-seven-year teacher in Shreveport, Louisiana. Her passion is teaching. Her problem was how to continue to make a difference in the lives of her students and the students that might not get the exposure that they deserve to explore STEM (science, technology, engineering, and mathematics) possibilities. Her solution: xSTREAM Learning, LLC in which the founder, Mrs. Connie Green designs learning camps for the inner-city kids to give them that exposure. Mrs. Green says, "The industrial revolution is over and our children need to be more creative and exposed more to STEM" if they are going to be successful.

It's my belief, she says, "That if students attend learning camp and get exposed to innovative learning activities, it will expand their learning to *Engage* the fun side of STEM, *Explore* the possibilities to become a Scientist, Tech Guru, Engineer, or Mathematician, and get *Excited* about changing their lives by just getting started." Mrs. Green deploys quadcopters and the iPhone in a revolution of her own to engage, explore, and excite students. I applaud Mrs. Green. Not only is she proof GeTN7 is on the right track, we agree the first step is to start. Until you can identify the pains and the needs, you shouldn't start your business. And if you do start, understand and accept you will start many times before you succeed.

The Questions You Need to Ask

Many people go to seminars and programs, and they say they want to start a business. One lady we're working with now wants to have her own salon. Our main question: "Why do you want to have your own salon? You know, you work in a salon now. What are you going to do differently?" You have to think like that, because there's a salon on every corner.

Why do you want to do it? What can you bring to this community that's different from all these others out there? When I say "community," I'm talking about where you are. It could be San Antonio. It could be Bexar County. It could be all of Texas. Or it could be all of the USA. *Remember, you start where you are.* Before you can grow globally, you have to start solving problems locally. That's what will help you shape your goal. That's what will show you a vision for your company. So start where you are. Go talk to some of the people around you in your neighborhood, people you know, people you meet. Ask them what's missing.

We Are Here

We have a presence online. And we are going into organizations that already exist. We don't compete against what's already there. Every city, including San Antonio, has organizations that are specifically set up and funded to help small businesses succeed. We go to them and partner with them. When we ask somebody, "What are you missing?" we already know the answer, because we've already done the research. But we want to help them with the missing parts.

Many people want to start a business. But they may not have done any research. We have. We can help them navigate the process before they spend thousands of dollars to find out they don't even have a problem to solve. Recently, we worked with a young man who wanted to get into the sneaker trade business. Don't laugh until you do the research, like we did: there is a huge market in collecting, trading, and selling *sneakers*.

I thought this was a crazy thing, until I looked into it. There are no regulations of course. It's a very busy segment online. People meet in parking lots trading sneakers—and making money! We researched the market, found out how big it is and where it was headed.

We got them started. When they became knowledgeable about what they wanted to do, they realized it was more work than they wanted to do. We helped them see this before they wasted thousands of dollars. We could have helped them come up with the capital, but it was still going to be a lot of work, and they simply weren't up for it.

We told them they had a great idea. But they didn't know what to do with it. We explained that you can't turn an idea into a business unless you are willing to partner with others who share your passion and can see your vision. If you don't believe you have to partner to get it done, that's your failure point right there. In this case, we saved him money by helping him see he couldn't succeed without thinking differently.

We look at ourselves more as advisers to help people do what they want to do, and help them understand exactly what that really means.

THREE IMPORTANT THINGS TO REMEMBER

1. Get started

Get started, because if you never start, you can never succeed. *Start where you are.*

2. Don't be anxious

If you don't get started, you cannot even think about succeeding. Some things are just out of your control. So? Use what you have and fail fast. Learning comes from your experiences. If you are afraid to fail, you won't learn what you need. None of us knows what we don't know. If you embrace failure as an opportunity to learn, then it's no longer failure.

3. Challenge and encourage others to be *doers*

Don't just theorize—*do something*. Climbing hills keeps you engaged and headed toward your dream. It helps you solve. It helps you be a part of the solution to what is perceived as a problem in society.

CHAPTER SEVEN

WHAT IS YOUR OX-GOAD?

Every experience, every success, every failure is designed to help you figure out your next move by learning from your last. This can be a difficult lesson, especially when failure is the teacher. It seems like such a weak instrument, yet it is certainly what works.

In helping others, we are very transparent about our own personal experiences—and we also use the experiences of those who paved the way before us. Often, we find examples of people in specific industries who did just that, who learned from their mistakes when they started out, then turned those mistakes into a tool that led to success. What did they do to succeed?

They failed first, then started again where they were. We hope that by sharing these kinds of stories we will help people find their way. I use a lot of biblical references, too. We're going to talk about what is blocking your path and how to get over, around, or under it.

As I think back about how my mantra has served me throughout my entire life, the theme of "starting where you are" has always been present, helping me meet challenges and finding a way to succeed, no matter the odds. For a long time, I thought the deck was stacked against me. I had no idea how I would ever escape that little cardboard-wall shack outside Coushatta. I didn't realize that was how God was pushing me, until I realized that my obstacles and my failures have made me who I am. I have my ox-goad and my faith, and that's all I need to defeat anything I encounter. I attacked diabetes that way. I attacked depression that way. I attacked poverty that way, and that's how I attacked fear, prejudice, and intimidation.

Sometimes, success unfolds so slowly in front of you that you don't realize what you have accomplished. My marriage and my life may not be where they ought to be, but, thank God, they're not where they used to be. It's all because I made a decision to start where I was, to embrace my talents and gifts, and get started. All I've ever had is what I've had. I use what I have every day and start where I am every morning, because every morning I realize that every day I've been through prepared me for

SHAMGAR

The story of Shamgar and his ox-goad illustrates my mantra: Start where you are and use what you have (Judges 3:31 as a starting point for my mantra). That verse in Judges is the only place in the Bible where Shamgar is mentioned. Of course, God uses a lot of ordinary people, but the story of Shamgar speaks to me. I think it can also speak to you, and to all of us.

Shamgar was called upon to save a desperate and depressed Israel from their threatening neighbors, the Philistines, who had robbed them of their defenses. Shamgar had nothing to use except his faith and an ox-goad, a kind of prod used to keep oxen in line. It was not much of a weapon, but it's all he had. He used that ox-goad wisely and well, and in the end, he killed 600 Philistines and saved Israel. He didn't freeze, or worry, or complain about how he was going to accomplish his mission. *He took what he had and started from where he was.* If you're facing a difficult task, but you don't know how to start, you can never succeed. Take up your ox-goad and get to work.

this day. And once this day is over, my experiences from today will prepare me for what I am to meet in the future.

They say that we overcome by the blood of the lamb, meaning Jesus Christ dying on the cross for us. But it's also the power of our testimony that helps us overcome—meaning that it's okay to share your story, even if it's a story of failure. When I was little, my mom used to tell us to share our story, because we never knew who it may help. Everybody has a story. As one marketing expert said, "It's the story that sells, persuades, enlightens, convinces." It's all in the story. It's your story that moves people to do things differently or encourages them to believe that they, too, can do something different.

Mantras Matter

Mantras have served a very special purpose throughout my life. When I was young, I didn't know what a mantra was. I didn't call it that. A mantra is just a saying or observation—three to five words that I use to help fuel who I am and how I approach my life and its challenges.

I was introduced to the idea of mantras by my business partner about five years ago. Before then it was just what I said to summarize a key belief at a pivotal point. For some time I used, "Anybody can be somebody." That was from when I was going through school. And when I graduated, I used it in my valedictorian speech. I lived with that mantra for years, until I went into the Air Force. In the Air Force, they called it a "motto." The Air Force mantra was the motto, "Fly, fight, win, and aim high." I mean, everybody knew that motto. It described who we were and how we acted. It's what we were about.

I gave a Federal Women's speech in 2006. The theme

that year was "women builders." So I titled my speech "Be Your Own Builder (for the over 40 group like me) or Owner-Builder-Network.com for those under 40)." That reflected the "start, do, build" mantra of the women builders. It described our ox-goad.

It was something I remembered from a sermon that I had heard back in Germany when I was depressed and very tired of Germany. I was working too hard. The pastor talked about Judges 3:31. He talked about starting where you are, using what you had, and doing what you can. God never gives us a burden heavier than what we can carry. I started embracing that and stopped worrying so much about the obstacles we all face. I asked, "Why are we trying to minister to 300 women when we have only five women who are actively engaged in ministry?" I said maybe God didn't want us to have 300 women. Maybe five is all we are supposed to have.

So in my talk, I said, "Let's just start where we are. Let's do smaller things. Let's use the five people that we have and we know we can count on, so we can do what we believe God wants us to do to build up the lives of others." I truly believed that. As I got ready to retire from the military, I looked back over my career and credited what I had achieved to my faith in God, my supportive family, and those friends that I had around me, because it takes more than one person to complete a twenty-year career in the military. I knew for sure that I had all of that support with me.

I got that from growing up and living the life God gave me. It wasn't something that the military taught me. My education and my military career provided the pieces, the ox-goads, the things that kept me together and kept me going. The "start, deal, build" mantra was a revision of the "start, use, do" mantra specifically written for women—the Federal Women Program—because their motto celebrated women builders.

As I talked to them that day, I told them about how they, too, could be builders—builders of their communities, of families, of businesses and homes. They could build websites, I said. They could do whatever they wanted to do.

To demonstrate that, I brought a hammer and a hardhat to the speech and talked about starting where they were, wherever they were in their careers or marriages or education, and how they could build upon that by using the time and talents they had been given. They had to get outside themselves to see that they were armed with the necessary ox-goads.

Career-building is about being able to do some of those

things that other people did not want to do. But *start, give, change* is more about who I am today. More than ever, I believe in starting where you are. I believe in giving, and in changing our circumstances. We can change diabetes. We can change our situation when we go through deaths in the family. We can change a bad marriage. I had to learn to allow God to work in me to change my attitude and my life. The things that used to bother me don't bother me anymore; I can look at my whole life in a healthier way and continue to move forward and be someone who is helpful in society and not someone who is all broken down.

Another mantra I love is, "Work while it is day. Nighttime comes when no man can work." As long as I'm alive, I want to be working. I want to be doing something that's worthwhile because there may come a time when I'm not able to, when darkness falls and someone may have to take care of me. That's when I'll ask, have I done enough? Have I done all I could do?

I'll find out, one day at a time. That's why I'm building a business of my own. That's why I'm trying to help others do the same.

AFTERWORD

I've changed a lot from that little girl growing up in Coushatta. I think I've traveled a great distance not only in physical miles, but also in life experiences. I think I have a healthier outlook on life now than at any time in my past. I'm not perfect, life's not perfect, but it doesn't have to be. I'm not rich, but I don't have to be. My son thinks I have a big house, but my house is not big. We are big in our home; we fill it with life and love and hope.

A plaque given to me by the men and women of the 52d Comptroller Squadron reads, "A hundred years from now it will not matter what your bank account was, the sort of house you lived in nor the kind of car you drove...but the impact you had on our lives will speak measures. Thanks for caring enough to make a difference, inspiring us to be the very best and teaching us the value of a true leader."

That's powerful. When somebody gives you something like that, they, too, are seeing you in a way that you didn't know yourself. Did you touch somebody while you were there? Was somebody else able to smile because you passed their way? That's success to me.

If my story has caused somebody to smile or to feel better about themselves, or to choose to live instead of sleeping, or to work while it is day, then I have succeeded in my purpose for writing this book.

I hope people will get up and take an assessment of themselves, look within themselves and ask, "What is my purpose? Who am I? How can I help? What can I do better?" Find out who you are and what your purpose is because, until you know your purpose, you're just putting in time. Pick up your goad and start where you are and say, "Today, I begin again. I will start just where I am. I will use what I have and I will do what I can, trusting God to do the rest. My story is not over."

ACKNOWLEDGMENTS

I'd like to thank my publishing team: Zach Obront, Hal Clifford, Denis Boyles, Jeremy Brown, Beth Richards, Lisa Amoroso, and Ian Claudius. I'm so grateful for their amazing teamwork.

ABOUT THE AUTHOR

MYRA EVANS-MANYWEATHER is a Program Manager for 502d Installation Support Group, Joint Base San Antonio, Lackland Air Force Base, Texas. She currently serves as an Executive Advisor for financial and human resources.

Ms. Evans-Manyweather entered the Air Force as a civilian in April 2006 as an over hire to serve as the Assistant Program Manager and Policy Advisor for the Implementation of the National Security Personnel System (NSPS). She was hired permanently as a Pay Pool Administrator and Compensation Manager in 2008. After NSPS was disbanded in 2010, she assumed her current role as Financial and Human Resource Advisor. Her valuable skills include financial management and budget execution, leadership development, team building, performance/process improvement, public speaking, facilitation, and small business ownership.

She has served as an Air Force Squadron Commander, Chief Financial Officer, Executive Assistant, Performance Management Advisor, Executive Compensation Manager, Executive Performance/Process Improvement Advisor, Executive Facilitator, Program Manager, and Project Manager. She has also served as a Human Resource Manager and a Pay Pool Administrator. Ms. Evans-Manyweather is currently a Certified Defense Financial Manager, and she owns her own business, Global e-Talent Network 7.0, LLC.

www.ingramcontent.com/pod-product-compliance
Lightning Source LLC
Chambersburg PA
CBHW060159050426
42446CB00013B/2910